FINDING FAITH

John Simmons

WESTBOW
PRESS®
A DIVISION OF THOMAS NELSON
& ZONDERVAN

This book is a work of non-fiction. Unless otherwise noted, the author and the publisher make no explicit guarantees as to the accuracy of the information contained in this book and in some cases, names of people and places have been altered to protect their privacy.

Scripture taken from the Holy Bible, NEW INTERNATIONAL VERSION®. Copyright © 1973, 1978, 1984 by Biblica, Inc. All rights reserved worldwide. Used by permission. NEW INTERNATIONAL VERSION® and NIV® are registered trademarks of Biblica, Inc. Use of either trademark for the offering of goods or services requires the prior written consent of Biblica US, Inc.

Scripture quotations taken from the Holy Bible, New Living Translation, Copyright © 1996, 2004. Used by permission of Tyndale House Publishers, Inc., Wheaton, Illinois 60189. All rights reserved.

Scripture quotations are from The Holy Bible, English Standard Version® (ESV®), copyright © 2001 by Crossway, a publishing ministry of Good News Publishers. Used by permission. All rights reserved.

New English Bible (NEB), Oxford University Press and Cambridge University Press ©1961, 1970

WestBow Press books may be ordered through booksellers or by contacting:

WestBow Press
A Division of Thomas Nelson & Zondervan
1663 Liberty Drive
Bloomington, IN 47403
www.westbowpress.com
1 (866) 928-1240

Because of the dynamic nature of the Internet, any web addresses or links contained in this book may have changed since publication and may no longer be valid. The views expressed in this work are solely those of the author and do not necessarily reflect the views of the publisher, and the publisher hereby disclaims any responsibility for them.

Any people depicted in stock imagery provided by Thinkstock are models, and such images are being used for illustrative purposes only.
Certain stock imagery © Thinkstock.

ISBN: 978-1-5127-0601-7 (sc)
ISBN: 978-1-5127-0602-4 (hc)
ISBN: 978-1-5127-0600-0 (e)

Print information available on the last page.

Library of Congress Control Number: 2015912221

WestBow Press rev. date: 10/19/2015

Contents

For Momma

During the almost 10 years I struggled with my addiction, you would tell me on a daily basis that I needed to pray and get help from God. I remember being so resistant to that idea. I always thought prayer, and God, didn't work for me. It wasn't until I was standing on the other side of my life looking back at where I used to be, that I was able to finally appreciate that you kept on telling me those things, even though I didn't always listen. Thank you for believing in me no matter what.

Thank you for helping me find faith. I love you.

Special Acknowledgements:

This book would not be possible without my wife.
I love you, Megan. You are my greatest blessing.
"Baby, Baby! The stars are shining for you!"

Kevin Eskew, thank you for your faith that I would find Christ, as well as, your insanely long nighttime conversations that led to many of the thoughts that I shared in these pages.

My family, thank you for the support you've shown me.
I feel it even though we are sometimes far apart.

I would like to openly thank Jesus. Thank you for listening when I reached out to you. I am astounded at what my life has become. I would've never picked this life for myself, but it has given me more joy than anything I would've chosen!

Preface

"Therefore, my brothers and sisters, make every effort to confirm your calling and election. For if you do these things, you will never stumble." **2 Peter 1:10 (NIV)**

I have never written a book. I rarely desire to read a book for enjoyment. I don't know why God asked me, of all people, to write one. All I know is that when He calls you to move, it is not usually to a seat you would normally take. He calls us to do extraordinary things. It is through these acts of unexplainable grace that God gets all the glory for our accomplishments. It is by no will of my own that this book will find its way into others' hands, but it is also by no "coincidence" either. I believe you were meant to have this in your hand. I have prayed for you, and I hope that you believe that these words will speak to you in a way that your heart can hear.

God has a great plan for your life. Finding faith to follow that plan is all you have to do to see it succeed. Once you begin to find the paths God has laid out for you, you'll never be the same. Once God reveals the bright future He has for you it will encourage you to wake up every day excited. Finding faith to follow God's will allows your thinking, and God-given gifts and talents, the ability to grow, and work together for His purpose. There is *no* limit to the growth and potential of your gifts when you are in God's will. God has the ability to make every person find what he or she has been looking for.

This book is designed to help encourage the growth of faith in many areas. It will discuss how we can find faith for God's purpose, find faith for our prayers to be answered, and find faith for overcoming problems. No matter which direction this book encourages you to go, it is my hope that it will help *you* specifically. God is the ultimate encourager, and I pray that you hear His voice speak to you in such a way you are able to understand while you read this. I believe that God will inspire a great promotion of faith for your life!

Finding faith isn't always easy, but it is *always* rewarding. God has blessings for all that believe. Those blessings can be handed out for any situation where faith is found. When you are able to find your faith daily, repeatedly, and without measure, then you will find God's abundant blessings in your life.

My Story of Finding Faith

"Repent of your sins and turn to God, for the Kingdom of Heaven is near." **Matthew 3:2(NLT)**

My name is John Simmons. I am a follower of Jesus Christ.

The first sentence has been true my whole life. The second sentence is much more important, but took almost thirty years to be true. I am only able to write this because Jesus saved me.

I was raised in St. Louis, Missouri. As a child, I occasionally went to a Baptist church that my grandmother took me to. When I was twelve I prayed for salvation at that church. I thought Jesus was my savior. One night soon after I was at home getting ready to go to bed, and I prayed to God that I would get off school the following day. I know it wasn't exactly a great prayer, but I was twelve.

The next morning I woke up to my mom coming into my room. I remember waking up and then looking at the clock. It was a little after nine in the morning. School started at 8 a.m. I was so excited! I must've gotten off of school. My prayer was answered, and God must have done it! My mom sat me up in bed. My excitement began to fade as I saw the look on my mom's face. You could tell she had been crying. She spoke gently, talked softly, and explained to me that my dad had a heart attack and passed away during the night. My life was shaken.

As the days, weeks, months, and years went by after my father's passing, I decided to blame God for what I thought He did. I had heard in church that God answered prayers in unexpected ways, and I definitely got an unexpected reason to be off of school. I also heard that God gives more than I could ever ask for. I prayed for one day off school and received many more. That moment was the starting point that led to my life away from Christ. Why would such a loving God answer prayers in such a terrible way? If that was how God worked, I wasn't going to pray to Him anymore. So I didn't.

I went on with my life, but I found myself on a longer leash after dad died. I spent a lot of time with friends who were older than me. Those friends influenced many decisions I made in life. I started drinking at fifteen years old and began smoking around the same time. I wouldn't say my friends and I were trouble makers; I would classify us more as typical teenagers. We were testing our limits, and trying to experience life by trial and error, but didn't get into any serious trouble.

I started working at a young age on a workers permit and found how much I liked having money. So I worked a lot more than most, if not all of the kids my age. During my senior year in high school, I was even in a program that allowed me to leave school every day to go to work. I worked as a cashier, cook, dishwasher, and eventually worked my way up to store manager at some of my jobs. I liked the freedom and opportunity that money provided me.

After high school I attended college for a couple years. I then dropped out to pursue a career in radio. I finished a radio trade school program in the area and found a job at the largest communications company in the state. I started "on the boards," which means I worked on a big control panel with lots of buttons and knobs to control the sound. I tried to make tapes and get promoted to DJ full time, but it never happened. I worked there for three years and never got to talk on the air more than a handful of times.

I began working as a store manager at a fast food restaurant and at the radio station concurrently. It was during this time that I was introduced to online poker because some of my older friends, and even members of my family, had started playing. The country was going through a "poker boom" as it was referred to. This was happening because ESPN had just started to air a contest on TV called the World Series of Poker. A man named Chris Moneymaker (his real name) won an entry into this contest and turned $40 into

$2.5 million by winning this tournament. After that everyone, including myself, wanted to be the next "moneymaker."

I began using the money from work to start playing online poker, just like many others that were around me. I had always really enjoyed poker and the different forms of it we would play around the kitchen table growing up. I thought online poker would bring back those memories and help pass times of boredom. I also thought I could win a couple of dollars and enjoy the feeling money gave me.

I started playing online poker around the time I was eighteen and played very modestly at first. I spent about $20 a month playing $5 tournaments with friends. That continued for a while. Then, I got a big jump in pay at my restaurant job. I was making close to $16/hour in 2002 plus another $10/hour at the radio station. My paychecks began to balloon. I didn't have a lot of expenses, and my left over money was beginning to increase significantly. Since I had no vision or place to put my money, I put it into my entertainment, which at the time was online poker.

For the first time, I started playing what are called "ring" games. They were different than the tournaments that I had been playing. In poker tournaments, like the one Chris Moneymaker won, I would pay an entry fee, and everyone that paid it would get the same amount of chips. I would then play until I won everyone else's chips or I lost my own. A "ring" game was a game I could play where I would put up my own money, and my chips would be equivalent to what I bought in for. I would then play against other players using their own money as chips as well. I could play as long or as often as I wanted. There were many different games with different stakes to play. The most important difference between tournaments and ring games was that there were no limits to how much of my money I could play with.

When I started online poker, I was playing $5 tournaments, and I would quit when they were finished. I was now buying into games for $50, and would buy more chips if I lost because I wanted to keep playing. While a tournament has a clear winner a ring, or cash, game does not. It might have several winners, or none. A ring game never stops, so I didn't either.

For my twenty first birthday I went to Las Vegas, and this is when I played poker in a casino for the first time. The games seemed similar to playing online, except it was against real life people. I was hooked. It was one of the most exciting moments of my life. I can't explain it, other than to say, I really felt like this was something I wanted to do often. I wanted to win money and have lots of it without really working for it.

When I got home, a friend told me that they had poker rooms at casinos in St. Louis. I went to check them out and saw the poker rooms were just like the ones I had been playing in Las Vegas. The only exception was that they were now down the street from my house. I started going to the casinos on my days off to play poker for hours and hours. One day at the casino, I talked to one of the older guys I knew from high school. He worked there as a poker dealer. He told me that they were hiring poker dealers and that they made $20+/hour. That sounded so exciting. As soon as I heard that, I knew that's what I wanted to do for a living. I applied for the job and was hired. I worked part-time at the casino and became immersed in that culture.

It was so different than anything I was used to. The environment was exhilarating, and I wanted more. Slowly, I began to spend more and more time playing cards. In 2004, I was offered full-time employment at the casino. I decided to leave both the restaurant and the radio station, jobs I was still working. Although I didn't realize it at the time, I was giving up on my dream to be on the radio, just to chase the fast and easy money of a casino lifestyle.

It didn't take long after that for my recreation to turn into something else entirely. I started spending every waking moment around poker. If I wasn't at work, I was at another casino playing, or I was at home playing online poker. The only time I wasn't playing was when I was sleeping.

I found out really early on that it takes a lot of money to fund this lifestyle. At first I was making so much that it didn't matter. It took a little while, but eventually I went through the money I had saved from working all those years. I then began to use credit cards to fund my habit. I would start blowing entire paychecks the day I got them just to support my gambling. I lost a lot of money. I didn't lose all of that because I was bad or because I couldn't win. I lost because I never stopped. I didn't know how to stop. Even if I were winning, I would stay until the money was all gone. A lot of times the only way I would ever leave is when the casino would close for the night. My addiction was not the money, but rather the high I felt while I was playing. The money was just the resource I needed in order to play it.

Early on, I went through a lot of money because I had no one to control my spending. I had great credit and was able to acquire credit cards with high limits. I would then max out that limit and go get another one. I built up massive amounts of credit card debt. When the credit cards stopped coming, I moved on to pay day loans, which are loans where I put my paycheck up as collateral. I would get a small loan for several hundred dollars at an outrageous interest rate sometimes as high as 675%. Once, I even sold the title to my car for $750, a fraction of what it was worth. I had dozens of these loans out across the city. I was using loans to pay off other loans.

Eventually my lending reached its limit, and I didn't know what to do. I had to tell my family for the first time about what I had been doing. It came as quite a shock, and it was a tough time in all our lives. On their instructions, I filed for bankruptcy at 22 years old. I signed a list to ban myself from gambling anymore at the Missouri casinos. They also had me enter into counseling, take medication to control my addiction, and started watching my bank accounts. I did, however, keep my job at the casino because it was so well paying, and I didn't have a better opportunity available.

The safety nets and precautions installed to keep me from gambling worked only for a little while. The lure of the casino world, and having to be around it every day at work, eventually sent me falling back into my addiction. This time I had to be more secretive because of all the attention my life was under from family and friends. I started taking creative steps to gamble. Since I was self-banned for life from going inside the casinos in Missouri, except to work, I took dozens of trips to visit out of state casinos. On my weekends off, I would travel to casinos up to 4 states away just to be able to play. It was around this time I began betting on sports as well. I found bookies were like credit cards because they would let me play without putting up the money first. It was an easy fix to the problem of not having money to gamble with!

This story repeats itself over and over again during the course of next seven years. I would gamble until I couldn't afford to anymore, and then I would ask others for help. I'd reach out to family, friends, acquaintances, or co-workers. It didn't matter to me who was bailing me out. I would then work as much as I could to recoup my losses and pay off my debts. During those days, I would hide myself wherever I was living when I was broke. I would sometimes go days and days without eating just because I spent all my money on gambling. This process was something I became very used to. I would gamble, lose, and then ask for help. After I had recovered my losses, I would begin to repeat this process again.

My addiction ruined over a decade of my life. I conservatively estimate that I lost more than $500,000 during that time. I lost many friends and relationships. I drove a wedge between myself and some of the members of my family. I made my mom cry time and time again. I was so miserable most of the time. I can't remember any memories I made that were worth keeping. I also can't find a picture of me from that time period because I avoided everyone. I was so ashamed of myself. I put on close to 100 pounds between the time when I started playing online poker and the height of my addiction.

Almost every night I would hope I wouldn't wake up. I did not want to live anymore. I had so many problems. I would never be able to solve them all. Everything I tried to do to win or to change my life around never worked. However, I never once during any of it thought that I should look to Jesus to solve my problems. I began to think I was meant to live this terrible life. I also thought I was a good person and didn't deserve this torture. I thought I was trying everything I could to be different, but for whatever reason, I just couldn't change. I was broken.

In the spring of 2012, I finally realized the depth of my problem, and I was ready to do the hard work to fix myself. I don't know what caused my desire for change exactly, but I was just done being broken. So in June, 2012, I entered a problem gambler rehabilitation program for the first time of my own free will. I had been through this program before and other programs like it. However, the times I had gone before were only at the request or insistence of my family or friends. Each of those times, I always wanted to be better, but I thought I was never going to be. Deep down, I also knew during each of those previous trips that I really didn't want to stop playing. I just wanted to stop losing.

I always thought if I were winning enough money that no one would consider my life a problem. It was never about the money though. My problem was my inability to stop. When I went back into counseling this time it was different, I was the one who wanted to go. I was really ready to get clean. I wanted my life to be different. I had suffered enough, and wanted to be free of my addiction.

Thirty days into the program, I received recognition for being clean. It felt really good to be recognized for something I did right. It had been so long since anyone told me I had done something good with my life. I wanted to be recognized again and prove to everyone watching me that I was better. I went sixty days clean, and I was feeling great. I received recognition again and was able to point at that milestone as a marker for success in my life. Not only that, but for the first time in almost a decade, I had money in the bank that wasn't earmarked for a gambling debt.

I was so excited after ninety days clean to go and be rewarded with honor and praise for what a good job I had done. When I went into my ninety day session I received my congratulations. After that, they told me my next milestone achievement wouldn't come again until I reached 6 months clean. So far we had celebrated my recovery every thirty days, and I had looked forward to that moment every month. How would I make it to six months clean without praise and honor to look forward to? It seemed so far away.

That is when I had the realization that something was wrong with me that I truly didn't understand before. I had just spent ninety days clean because I wanted to make my life better. However, at no point during those ninety days did my desire to gamble go away. I was fighting off constant cravings and pushing through tough days only to get to that achievement ceremony. I knew there was an underlying issue. I still didn't want to stop. Rehab, I thought, was supposed to make me want to stop gambling. I thought it was supposed to fix me. Rehab helped me keep my focus on other things, but it didn't make me want to stop. My desire never left me. Yes, I didn't want my actions to hurt anyone including myself anymore, but that wasn't enough.

When I told my counselor what I was thinking about, I was told that rehab doesn't fix you, it just helps you control the problem by focusing on living one day at a time. After hearing that, all I could think about was what a struggle it had been to get through each day. I felt like it was harder trying not to gamble than it would've been to gamble and deal with the consequences. It took all of my effort and focus to stay clean. I wasn't able to focus on work or people. All I thought about was trying to distract myself with food, cigarettes, or TV. That is not a life that is any better than a life of constant gambling. I wanted so badly to be different than I had been.

My thoughts began to race as I sat in that ninety day meeting. "Why can't this desire go away? Will I just have to live like this my whole life? I won't be able to live that way? Six months is so far away. Why am I like this?"

When I walked out of my ninety day celebration, I got in my car, and immediately placed the biggest bet I had made in years. I followed that bet by going on an eight day bender. I spiraled out of control going through every cent I had saved. I sold anything of worth I still had and burned up all the credit with the bookies I could get.

The bender came to an end September 8, 2012. That night ended with another lost bet. I had exhausted all of my resources. I was at the end of my rope, out of money, and out of hope. This experience was not new to me; I had many nights exactly like this in the past. The only thing that was different this time was how hopeful I had been just days before about getting myself a better life. I was distraught. I didn't know why I was like this. I didn't want to be this person anymore. I was done.

So I went into my room and was unsure what to do. I had thoughts of suicide. I had thoughts of running away. I had thoughts of wishing I could take back the last eight days. I had thoughts about how none of the choices I made ever worked. I didn't know why life why so hard for me.

In that moment, I decided to pray to God.

I hadn't talked to God in a long time. I wasn't sure how I was supposed to even talk to God or even if I still really believed in Him or not. I said these words "God, if you are real, I need you to give me a hope for the future. I can't live like this anymore."

That was it. No long winded prayer of bargaining. No real thought that it would work. I didn't know if God heard me, or if He even cared about me anymore.

He did.

As soon as I finished saying those words out loud, I began to hear a sentence repeat over and over in my mind. This was not my own thought. I thought I was going crazy at first. There is no way it could've been something I was thinking. It didn't make any sense to me. This is what God said to me that night over and over and over again, like a CD turned up on loud that was stuck on repeat in my mind:

"The Kingdom of Heaven is upon you."

I thought I was going crazy! I wondered what that phrase meant. I didn't realize it was God. I walked out of my bedroom to get away from those thoughts. When I walked into my living room my eyes were drawn to the bookshelf, which had the Bible that belonged to my dad on it. I felt compelled to open it. I didn't know why. I hadn't opened a Bible in close to sixteen years. I opened to the first page of the New Testament and started reading the book of Matthew. When I read the third chapter of Matthew, all of a sudden my world went from dark to light.

I read this in my Dad's Bible:

"Repent, for the Kingdom of Heaven is at hand."
Matthew 3:2 (NEB)

I freaked out and started to cry. I didn't know that was in there. I hadn't opened a Bible or seriously thought about God in sixteen years. Yet somehow, I was reading a verse that was on repeat in my own head. This was a verse told to the people to lead them to salvation. God had just told me that I repented and was now a part of His kingdom. God knocked me down with His presence in that moment!

I started to read more and saw the phrase "Kingdom of Heaven" said many more times throughout the chapter. As I read the words in the Bible, words that were hard to understand suddenly made sense to me. I couldn't read the Bible fast enough. I was thirsty for these words. I had an understanding about life that I had never felt before. I knew everything just changed.

Not a single moment in my life will be more important than that. It became the moment I knew God was real. It became the moment I knew my life was different. It was the night I was going to give up completely. It was the night I thought I would die; instead, I was reborn.

I soaked up the Bible like a sponge, but I had lots of questions. I reached out to the only person I knew with an understanding of the Bible and asked him a million questions about God, Jesus, and the Holy Spirit. I could not get enough. I read a lot; when I stopped reading, I started listening to pastors and Christian talk radio. I needed more information. For months, every second of my waking day was spent soaking my life in God's light.

Eventually, the dust settled on my bender. I recovered financially. Things were different now though, and I knew it. The process of gamble, lose, ask for help, recover, and repeat was broken. I began a personal relationship with Jesus Christ that night. We began to walk together, and He began to teach me, train me, and give me knowledge about His Kingdom.

Pretty early on in my studying, I found out why I felt helpless to stop gambling, and why I couldn't feel better about my life. I had that feeling because I had a giant hole inside me before I found Christ. We are all born with a giant hole, not literally but figuratively, that can only be filled by Jesus. Every single person on Earth has a desire to fill that hole with something, but it is designed to be filled by the love of Jesus. Every single one of us needs to fill that hole. No one is exempt. We can't help it. If we decide not to fill it with Jesus we can only fill it with two others things. We can only fill that hole with pleasure, pain, or both.

We will do whatever it takes to make ourselves feel better, or worse, to distract us from the displeasure we have from a life without Jesus. That is why all nonbelievers find themselves facing battles they can't seem to win, addictions they can't beat, and an overall sense of not having joy. Some people might try and fill their hole by buying or collecting a lot of stuff. Others will try and fill their hole with the lives of their children, and some might find a bottle, a pill, or a person to distract them from the emptiness they feel from a life without Jesus.

When Jesus filled that hole for me, I clearly focused my attention on God, and in return, I found out that He focused His attention on me, too. He began to clean up my life, although it didn't happen overnight. In fact, I gambled several times *after* I was born again. I never stopped trying to get closer to God, and he never stopped teaching me and giving me grace for everything I asked for.

I have now been clean for the longest period of my adult life *and* the compulsion to gamble that seemed to never leave me is now gone! That relief is something that can never be accurately described by words. I didn't do anything to make that go away. I didn't will it away, or even believe that I could ever lose it. Jesus took that from my life. His grace covers that for me. I no longer am fighting a losing battle with that enemy. Jesus is my shield.

I started writing this book one year after I was born again, and my personal relationship with Jesus Christ in that time has led to deliverance from my addictions and a complete change in my life. The number of changes God has made in my life since I started my walk is uncountable. They are too immeasurable to be thought of as "willpower." I tell people who don't believe it was Jesus that caused my change to remember that I didn't have enough willpower to stop smoking or gambling before, so they shouldn't think that I suddenly have it now.

My relationship with Jesus was the only thing I changed in my life, and if Jesus is the only change that happened in my life moments before hundreds of other changes took place, He is the reason for all the changes. My freedom from addiction is not a coincidence, and that is the truth. Jesus saved me! He saved me from more than Hell, too. He saved me from my old life and from all the struggles that tried to destroy me.

Over the course of my walk, God called me to quit my job as a poker dealer to follow Him and start a ministry called Testimony House. Testimony House focuses on sharing testimonies with non-believers so that they can see the love of Christ on the lives of believers, and seek that out for their own life.

Testimony House is also a Christian learning center dedicated to helping believers increase their production in the Kingdom by learning and walking in their gifts *and* talents to follow God's vision, or purpose, for their lives. God made us all to do something very specific. We need to believe in that, *and* ask Him to reveal it to us in the same way we believe in and ask for salvation.

This is my role in the body of Christ. I am meant to share Christ with others. That includes my work through Testimony House, at church, at home and through my writings. I am not overly qualified. I am no better Christian than any other. I just am trying to live a life in service of Him. Jesus changed my life in ways I didn't even think were possible. I feel more blessed on my worst day now than I did on my best day during my struggles. It is my desire to live my life sharing the love that Jesus has for me with others. It is my hope that people hear the message of Christ through me, and turn to Him, so they may experience this epic change for themselves.

I am sharing my story so that many can see the impact of God in my life, and prayerfully choose Christ. Remember: I was a poker dealer for almost ten years, had not opened a Bible in over a decade, and struggled with severe addiction and an intense depression. If it is possible for my life without hope and a future to turn around, I believe your life can change for the better as well.

God is real. Jesus Saves. All you have to do is find faith.

Part One:
Introduction to Faith

Faith is the Source of Joy

"I pray that God, the source of hope, will fill you completely with joy and peace because you trust in him. Then you will overflow with confident hope through the power of the Holy Spirit." **Romans 15:13 (NLT)**

Have you ever shared your heart with someone and told them that "you just want your life to be happy?" If so, what did you say it for? Was it because bad times hit you or because you found yourself dealing with a constant or lingering depression? Did you use this sentence because you are lonely due to a lack of a relationship or maybe because you are in one that is broken? Did you use this phrase to describe the way you feel about being in a poor financial situation? **There are many reasons to be unhappy; however, finding faith in God is the only way to find complete joy in your life.**

When we use the statement, "I just want my life to be happy," it is blanketed over our whole life but, generally, doesn't apply to every area in it. In other words, we may be upset because of a relationship problem, but this one instance has made us feel like our whole life is in trouble, even though it has nothing to do with other areas like family, money, or our job. What we need to learn about happiness is that it is only connected to the current situation we are experiencing. The truth about happiness is that is not actually what we should be looking for.

Happiness is a fleeting feeling that comes and goes with our situations. We can be happy we were invited to a party, got a promotion, or found $20 in our pockets, but situations do not supply our entire *life* with happiness.

Joy is what supplies our life with happiness. Joy, as defined by thefreedictionary.com, is intense or exultant happiness; a condition of happiness. When we say, "I just want my life to be happy" what we really mean is, "I want my life to be joyful!" Joy is a condition of happiness. When we have joy, it means happiness is a part of us. Joy is an intense feeling of happiness that surrounds all our situations, and not just one moment of our lives. When we have joy, happiness is blanketed over our entire life.

How do we find joy? Romans 15:13 tells us that joy comes from the Lord. In fact, the Bible tells us in this verse that God can *fill* our life with joy, peace, and hope. The Bible also says we can receive these things by putting our trust, or our faith, in the Lord.

Faith in the Lord is what brings joy, peace, and hope into our lives!

If we are unhappy, it is because something happened to us that we didn't want to happen. Unhappiness can be caused by a number of reasons including a break-up, firing, or because our car broke down. If we are depressed, it is likely because many of those situations have begun to pile up, and because of our circumstances, we now have a dim outlook on the future. Depression happens because the sum of all those problems creates an unsolvable puzzle in our mind. We think because there are so many problems to solve, that there is no way they all will be solved. Depression is the result that happens when we look at our future and do not see ourselves overcoming our problems.

Why do we get depressed when we think our future is dim? Romans 15:13 tells us that joy comes from faith. Faith is the belief that we have a blessed future that comes from God. Our level of joy comes from where we think our future is headed. If we think our future will be bad we become depressed, and when we think God will make it good, we become joyful.

Imagine you are about to go on a vacation. During the weeks and months before your trip, you are extremely happy and excited to go. You tell all your friends; you plan different tourists spots to visit; and you are counting the days until you will be off work for a while. You are so excited; you are *expecting* a great trip; and you've told everyone how great it is going to be. What you are actually doing is exhibiting faith in this situation. Joy comes from faith, and having faith is why you get so excited to go on vacation.

What we don't do during the pre-trip excitement and planning period is to dwell on any idea of something negative happening. We won't spend time before our vacation thinking, or daydreaming, about the possibility that we might get stuck at the airport, that we could lose our luggage, or it'll cost us way more than we are able to spend. No one wants to ruin the thought of the future vacation by believing that bad things will happen. However, this is what our "non-vacation" attitude about life looks like. In life, we tend to focus on all the bad things that will prevent our life from being a success, rather than planning out exciting things to do along the way while we are there.

In order to start saying, "My life is full of joy," instead of saying, "I just want my life to be happy," we need to have a bright outlook on the future by making sure God is our source of hope. We find faith in God by having a positive expectation that what's coming ahead will be handled by Him, and not dwelling on the negative circumstances that might happen.

Faith in God=hope for our future=joy.

God promises us throughout the Bible that living a life with faith will bring our lives *more* than we could ever ask or think (Eph. 3:20). We can have all our heart desires when we use faith correctly for His purpose (Ps. 37:3-5). It's not always easy, and sometimes even if we're in faith, we may get unexpected, or seemingly undesirable, results. Faith in God provides hope, and even in undesirable situations hope can get us to the other side of unhappiness.

Finding Faith will show us that our struggles may be uncommon; however, faith in God is the common solution. Faith in God can do big things like cure the worst illness, and turn around the worst life, but it can also pay our car bill, make sure we have food, or allow us to go on that vacation.

Faith isn't just the answer for the big things. Faith in God is the answer to *everything*!

Faith is a Choice

"Faith is the confidence that what we hope for will actually happen; it gives us assurance about things we cannot see."
Hebrews 11:1 (NLT)

Hebrews 11:1 tells us that God's definition of faith is having an assured belief that great things will happen when we expect them to. The opposite of faith, or doubt, means if we are expecting things not to work out then they probably won't. In life, we *always* believe in one of these two things, either yes or no. Our lives are filled with moments where we decide that something is either right or wrong, enough or not enough, if it's going to work or if it's not. We are always making a choice, and even indecision is a decision.

Choice is our God-given right on this planet. We get to choose if, when, and how we believe in God. We get to choose the field in which we will work. We also get to choose if we will obey laws. Today, we may have already chosen something to eat, a show on TV to watch, or a radio station to listen to in the car. We *always* have a choice; yes or no, more or less, stay or go, follow or lead, sit or stand, speak or listen. Choice has been given to us to use however we want. These decisions will construct the path of our life. The ripple effects are endless. Our choices will also affect those close to us, and sometimes those not close to us.

The best possible outcomes our life can take are options we don't pick for ourselves. It sounds wrong, but it's not. God gave us the gift to make choices, but in every situation He also leaves us with the opportunity to choose a better option. Every choice we will make in our lives comes down to this:

Do we take God's path or our own?

In many situations, we believe our way *is* the better choice. We think the desires of our heart are always guiding us to make good decisions. We think our minds have constructed the best possible way for us to be happy. It's simply not true. Choosing our own way may bring temporary happiness but we need joy, not just happiness, and we cannot create a path for our life that leads to true joy without God.

God made a plan specifically for us, but He won't force us to take it. If we decide to take God's path it will require us to take faith with us. We were also born with different gifts and talents to achieve God's plan for us. No matter when we get on our God designed path, the Bible says He redeems lost time (Joel 2:25). We don't ever have to believe that we are "too late" to receive the plans God laid out for us. Finding faith is about more than just finding God, it is about finding a way to make the better choice—which is always taking God's path for our lives. Faith is about allowing God to improve our future.

When we find faith, we are letting our beliefs define our outcome, not letting our outcome define our beliefs.

Faith in Christ Leads to Salvation

*"And the judgment is based on this fact: God's light came
into the world, but people loved the darkness more than
the light, for their actions were evil. All who do evil hate
the light and refuse to go near it for fear their sins will be
exposed. But those who do what is right come to the light
so others can see that they are doing what God wants"*
John 3:19-21 (NLT)

Salvation is the ultimate choice. Will we choose salvation, by
believing in the life, death, and resurrection of Jesus Christ as
payment for our sins, or will we believe *anything* else? We get to
make that choice, but we didn't get to choose the options. God chose
the path our faith must take to reach salvation, but we will choose
whether or not He knows better than us. We will decide during the
course of our lives whether constructing our own path for eternity
is better than following the one Jesus created for us.

**God is real; He created the Earth and all of us on it.
God sent His son, Jesus, down to Earth to live a life as a
man, so that we could be redeemed through Him. Those
that confess and believe Jesus lived a sinless life, died, and
was resurrected as payment for our sins will have eternal life
(Rom. 10:9). None of the faith learned to use, grow stronger
in, or overcome with, will matter if we don't find faith for
salvation.**

John 3:19-21 speaks to the difficulty we will have finding faith
for salvation through Christ. Jesus, who is the light of the world,

exposes our sin, and man will always refuse to go near Jesus because they do not want their sins exposed. However, those that do find faith in Jesus as their Savior will seek out His light, so that their lives can be sanctified and they will benefit from the free gift of God – which is eternal life through Christ (Rom. 6:21-23).

Finding faith for salvation is simple, but it isn't easy because we have to fight against our sinful nature, attacks from the enemy, and doubt. John describes that dual nature we will fight in these verses. Our sinful nature is at battle against our spiritual nature. However, once we find faith for salvation, we become a powerful tool in God's armory, and our lives become a testimony to the power that a relationship with God has.

God made it easy to receive salvation. All we have to do is confess with our mouths and believe in our hearts that Jesus is Lord (Rom. 10:9). However, the enemy makes it very difficult to get to a place in our hearts where we will believe we need salvation. We get attacked in many ways, and we often believe, just as I did before I was saved, that our way is rational thinking. We don't even know we are being blinded until we accept the gospel as our way of thinking. Our sinful nature tries very hard to convince our minds that the gospel is not true.

What is the truth?

All of us are born without salvation (Ps. 51:5). At some point the gospel message of salvation will be shared with all of us (Matt. 24:14). Many will face challenges to find faith in it (Luke 13:24).

Our challenges to find salvation will be many, and each challenge can provide our minds with enough doubt to take up the space where faith needs to go. When we are full of doubt, we prevent faith from occurring and, in turn, prevent salvation from occurring.

For believers and unbelievers finding faith is hard. Believers have a hard time finding faith for a number of things like blessings, healings, and miracles. Unbelievers, on the other hand, and we all were at one point, have to start finding faith in the hardest spot to find it. For me, remembering how difficult my journey to finding faith in Christ was should make my journey of finding faith for Him to answer my prayers like a walk in the park!

These are just some of the challenges facing believers, and unbelievers, in their journey to finding faith in Christ:

- Some will have a hard time believing God exists.
- Some will have a hard time believing Jesus was the Son of God.
- Some will have a hard time believing God has a plan for them.
- Some will have a hard time believing that the only way to heaven, or eternal life, is through Christ.
- Some will have a hard time believing God will show up for them.
- Some will believe that God's too busy to be concerned for them.
- Some will have a hard time believing God is going to answer their prayers.
- Some will have a hard time believing God loves them.

I believe you are on that list somewhere, maybe even multiple times. We all are. If having faith in God was so easy to do, we wouldn't need so many scriptures in the Bible teaching us about it.

Wherever you find yourself on this list, I want you to know, you are *not* alone. Many people are facing the same battle in their minds. Thankfully, those battles are won when we ask God for help. God is always with you and ready to reveal Himself to those that ask (Matt. 7:7).

Each of us finds faith for salvation differently because we all have different doors holding us back from Christ. God speaks to us all individually to tell us where we can find the keys in our heart to unlock salvation in our own lives. No two testimonies of finding faith for salvation will ever be the exact same, but they will *all* include the requirement that God tells us about Himself in His Word – which is the belief in Jesus Christ as Lord.

"For God so loved the world that he gave his one and only Son, that whoever believes in him shall not perish but have eternal life." **John 3:16 (NLT)**

Our salvation and the faith God asks us to use to receive it is easy to understand, but it isn't always easy to do. Similarly, it is easy to say, "I'm going to quit smoking," but it is much harder to find ourselves doing so. Any situation where we have to change provides difficulties, whether it's quitting smoking, finding salvation, losing weight, or finding a job. Every change presents certain challenges, but God has the solution for them all.

Common themes run throughout many testimonies of believers. All of them had a change of thinking. All of them were able to understand what they were doing wasn't working. They gained the knowledge that God is all loving, and they wanted to experience that love for themselves.

Finding faith to overcome the difficulty to find salvation begins with knowing God will reveal Himself to us. God's plan is for everyone to hear the gospel and hear it in a way they are able to understand and receive it. God knows better than any of us what works for one person won't always work for another. Once we hear the message of the gospel, then it becomes our choice to put our faith in that message or not.

Salvation is not a requirement of God for our lives; it is a choice. Choosing God's way of doing things or our own is the choice we all must make. Thankfully, God inspires us to find faith in Christ through His Word, the church, and through the testimonies of believers. We can choose one of those methods to find faith, or we can ignore them, but through faith in Jesus Christ is the only way to be saved.

"There is salvation in no one else! God has given no other name under heaven by which we must be saved." **Acts 4:12**

Faith Looks Forward

"For nothing is impossible with God." **Luke 1:37 (NLT)**

Our life is strung together by thoughts, steps, and actions that impact our future. With God, or without Him, every life is designed to focus its energy on the future. We are all looking ahead at something, good or bad. We even use the term "looking forward" to mean we are excited about something in our future. We often will say "I'm not looking forward to that" when something in our future is unappealing, but when describing events in our future that are exciting we might say, "I'm looking forward to seeing that new movie," "I'm looking forward to being a parent," "I can't wait until I get that new car," or "I'm pumped to start my new job."

Our plans and goals for tomorrow design the steps we take to get there. This is where faith begins.

Faith is not the throw away word used to describe wanting success in unlikely events. Unbelievers over the years have taken the word faith, which is a powerful word and tool for the kingdom of Heaven, and depreciated its value. Faith isn't just a word used by irrational people to make sense of what they don't understand, or a word used to find hope in situations that have absolutely none. Faith is the powerful way for us to "look forward" to our future and find victory all along our path.

When truly walking in faith we should be "looking forward" to *every* moment of our future with the same excitement, and expectation, that we use for things like a vacation or a new home.

We should believe that when God's will is being done in our lives all situations will work out for the best, including ones that don't look like fun to deal with, or ones that we believe are going to result in an undesirable outcome. I understand that many would say that is a waste of energy and/or hope. I mean why would we *really* believe that a dire or undesirable situation can provide a desirable outcome?

We believe bad situations can turn good because in Luke 1:37 it says, "nothing is impossible." Faith in God to turn things around for our good is necessary to prevent any negative outcome from actually coming true (Rom. 8:28). We *always* have one of two choices. We can either face a terrible situation with faith or without faith. We have the choice to turn all of the realities in our life into moments we are "looking forward" to.

Those who have faith in Jesus are promised by God to have an abundant life, and a future that has immeasurable blessings (John 10:10, Matt. 6:33). Faith in God promises us all these things, and without faith, life becomes full of unrelenting questions as well as desires that lead us to constantly change our minds. Without faith, we may find ourselves asking, "Am I doing the right thing," or "Do I need to be somewhere else in my life?" We question our choices because we want to find joy in our lives, and we are often unsure about which road takes us there. Choosing to find the faith to walk down God's path for our life is the only road we can use to get to joy. Knowing our life is on God's path to joy is something we can be "looking forward" to.

Part Two: Keys of Faith

Finding Keys of Faith

"And I will give you the keys of the Kingdom of Heaven. Whatever you forbid on earth will be forbidden in heaven, and whatever you permit on earth will be permitted in heaven." **Matthew 16:19 (NLT)**

Jesus is talking to Peter in this verse. Jesus is giving Peter instructions on what power he will have on Earth after Jesus leaves it. Jesus uses the simple idea of handing over the keys because He knows we use keys to unlock things, get access to items that we didn't have before, and they allow us to enter into places we couldn't earlier. Peter needed great faith to follow the path Jesus was asking him to walk. Jesus left Peter the keys because he needed to be equipped for his journey to get into the places Jesus needed him to go. Keys are as essential to us today as they were then, and we will use keys throughout this book to unlock our faith.

Have you ever misplaced your keys right before you have to leave? Did you run around frantically and check all the possible locations you might have left them? Did you feel panicked and desperate to find them? Did you find yourself saying or thinking things like, "Where did I put those keys," "I can't believe I lost them," or you may even turn to asking other people, "Have you seen my keys?"

These are all common thoughts and reactions for us to have when we lose our keys. However, we are probably never going to stop and ask the question, *"Why* do we need our keys?"

We won't stop to think why we need our keys because we already know the answer. We know we can't lock or unlock the doors to our house or start our cars without a key. When our keys are with us, we are never worried. When we lose our keys, however, it becomes our number one priority and worry to find them. We will likely think, "I *have* to find my keys; I *need my keys.*" When we lose our keys, we will become focused and fixated on that problem.

A second ago, before we lost our keys, we were worry free, and had it all together. Now, our life has this tiny problem, and everything is seemingly falling apart. Now that we know we have a problem, we are concerning all of our efforts to finding its solution. All we can think about is finding our keys *right now*!

It is very common for us to lose our keys. It is also very common to lose our faith. Unlike our keys, however, when we lose our faith we don't realize we lost it until we are too far away to turn back and get it. Our faith, and our keys, share many similarities, and we should see our faith as important a thing to carry around with us as our keys.

How is our faith like our keys?

- **Faith holds a very important and vital role in our everyday life.**
- **When faith is working it opens and locks doors, gets us where we need to go, and it provides security to our brain that everything is all right.**
- **When we lose our faith we become frantic, one track minded, and are focused on a problem that we can't seem to fix.**
- **Faith is very hard to find when it is lost.**

Have you ever been driving down the highway and checked to see if your keys are still in the ignition? Absolutely not! The car wouldn't run if the keys were out of it.

This is a way of visualizing how Jesus told us our faith is supposed to work. We need our faith just like we need our keys. There is no need to see our keys in the ignition to know they are working, and we don't need to see all the work God does behind the scenes to make sure our faith is working, either. When we find faith, it is the key to our ignition of God's life for us, and we will be driving into our abundant future.

Using Keys to Unlock Opportunity

"There is a wide-open door for a great work here, although many oppose me." **1 Corinthians 16:9 (NLT)**

When contemplating a change in life, the first step is usually the hardest. It becomes even more challenging to step out when making big life decisions when they impact the future of others close to us. Trying to wrap our head around all the possibilities, and all of the "what ifs" becomes a seemingly endless proposition.

Paul uses 1 Corinthians 16:9 as an illustration for how great an opportunity Christians had to reach people in places that had yet to hear the gospel. Paul also tells us that there will be opposition to that great work. Paul shared the gospel with thousands of people, but was thrown in prison, and beaten many times because of his faith. Even though God has given us wide open doors to walk through we need to remember that there are forces trying to get us off God's path for our lives. It is our job to use faith when opening those doors, and believe when we walk through them we will find ourselves receiving God's blessings.

Opening a door into a new place can be concerning. When we are trying to make any change, doing something new, or allowing ourselves the opportunity to grow, it can be a difficult step to take. When we are doing something we're not sure of but believe is best, it means we are taking steps of faith.

Testimony

I used to have this big problem going into new places. I might have gone as far as to describe it as a fear or a phobia. When I had to walk into a new place I would often do several things to get out of it or change the circumstances. I was terrified to meet new people. I didn't like going into buildings I had never been in before or finding places I needed to be inside that building. Going to a new DMV and applying for a job were especially hard situations for me. I would often postpone appointments with doctors, or meeting with friends in places I wasn't familiar. Postponing the inevitable somehow gave me a little relief and helped my mind prepare for what I was about to do.

I thought I could mentally prepare for brand new moments in life if I had more time to think about it. Actually, I made myself more worried. It was like an infection I didn't take care of, and it got worse. Doubts and worries played havoc in my mind. However, when these brand new moments did happen, I would be very excited with the outcome and would even get angry at myself later because I didn't do it sooner.

It wasn't until I found Christ that I realized how great things can happen in new places. Christ took that fear from me to make change and do new things. My faith was the key to opening doors in my life that were absolutely locked before Christ. My faith was the key I used to walk into a new church desiring revival. My faith was the key to a door that sent me to a multi church fellowship where I met my wife. My faith was the key to taking a job that was instrumental in the publishing of this book.

Finding faith can be uncomfortable sometimes. When we are trying to find faith, the enemy will bring feelings of uneasiness, dread, doubt, and worry. We might think, "What if it doesn't work out," "What if they don't like me," or "What if I say or do something stupid or make a mistake?"

All of these examples are perceived rational thoughts about new situations that have kept us from places we wanted to go, and possibly kept us from places we were *meant* to go.

There is no need now to worry about what we used to do or how we used to react to situations of change or newness. Instead, we can concentrate our focus on changing our worry into hope, and instead of doubt, we can find faith in God to guide our decisions. However, we must train ourselves, through repetition, in order to consistently do new things in order to receive all the blessings God has in store for us through those moments.

Opening a door is our opportunity to make a change. That new door can sometimes look difficult to open. It's not as tough as it looks when we use faith. Faith, remember, is our key. Faith opens up God's desired changes to happen in our lives. Without faith, those doors will stay shut, and opportunities will be lost all because we didn't have our keys of faith. Change is the door we need to walk through in order to achieve that positive future. Faith is the key that unlocks it.

The following are keys of behavior we can exhibit that allows our faith to become a functional tool we use every day. When we carry these keys with us, we will find ourselves equipped with the tool we need to open doors and to make our future better. Our joy is directly correlated with the vision we have for the future God has for us. We can't have a bright future without first finding the faith in God to believe that we can have it.

Keys to Unlocking Opportunities

- **Rely on the Lord**
- **Don't Be Discouraged**
- **When God Asks, Take a Big Leap**

Rely on the Lord

Before Paul opened the doors to share Christ in new places he needed to rely on the Lord to know where to go, when to get there, and what to do when he got there. Paul told God what he desired to happen by praying that everyone he talked to would be reconciled to God (2 Cor. 5:20). Paul prayed without ceasing, and prayed for a multitude of requests (1 Thess. 5:17, Eph. 6:18). He maintained a reliance on the Lord for all things.

When we are facing a new door to open, we must lean on God for all things. We can be honest with Him about how we are feeling and what we desire to happen. All we need to do is ask for God to supply us with peace, grace, and mercy when entering into something. It may seem uncomfortable, but walking through doors leads to blessings. Allowing ourselves to fully rely on the Lord in all things will give us the strength to push doors open.

Don't Be Discouraged

Not every person we meet, opportunity we receive, job offer we take, doctor's appointment we go to, or date we go on will end exactly as we want them to. These moments can be very disappointing. That leads to worry and doubt because we might think, "If it was from God it should have worked out." However, we don't always know God's plan.

God may be using this moment to test our perseverance, in order to see if we will get back up, and try something again even though it failed the first time. God may be testing our patience to wait expectantly for the right person He needs us to meet, the right job He wants us to get, or the best opportunity He wants us to receive, to finally arrive.

There is no path that follows God's will that is void of twists and turns. We can't let discouragement break down our faith. God has a plan for our lives. Discouragement, like Paul tells us in 1 Corinthians 16:9, is just one of the many oppositions coming against us to try and stop us from using God's plan in our life. God will direct our steps and guide our paths, but we must keep hopeful in our expectations, regardless of our circumstances (Prov. 3:5-6).

When God Asks, Take a Big Leap

God will ask us to use our faith as a key to unlock doors of opportunities. If we want to see God's blessings come from open doors, we will need to walk through them. If we are unsure what door God is calling us to open, we will need to challenge ourselves to open them all.

We open doors by not postponing or cancelling anything on our calendar. We open doors by going to places we are invited to go. We open doors by helping someone who asks for help. Fear and doubt can't be the reason we aren't opening doors. When we faithfully open a door God has put in our path, it will likely end with a great result we never knew we wanted to get.

Sometimes God tells us what door to take, and many times He just puts the door in front of us to see if we *will* take it.

God told me to take the door to ministry and put the door in front of me that led to my wife. God called Paul to share the gospel in cities that didn't want him there, but Paul used his faith to open those doors even though he was unwanted. The people who found Jesus in those places were blessed because Paul opened the door to their city. Our lives will be full of doors to open, so we shouldn't be afraid to take that big leap, and go into places we may feel uncomfortable, unworthy, or unnecessary because those opportunities could lead to a better future for our lives and, possibly, the lives of others.

Finding Faith from Relationships

"Direct your children onto the right path, and when they are older, they will not leave it." **Proverbs 22:6 (NLT)**

Our relationships are a blessing from God. God says it is not good for a man to be alone. He asks us to be fruitful and multiply and also blesses those who fill their lives with children (Gen. 2:18, 9:7, Ps. 127:5). Relationships with family, friends, classmates, and co-workers will surround us throughout life, and they will shape who we are, how we act, and how we live.

Proverbs 22:6 says when we teach children what is right it will stay with them throughout their lives. This means our childhood has a giant influence on how we walk in faith as adults. God gave us the opportunity to learn how to rely upon our faith as children because we *all* relied entirely on others to provide for us in our early lives. That high level of faith can begin to lessen over time, as we begin to rely more and more on ourselves in life. This verse reminds us that even if our faith isn't as high as it once was, we now know it is possible to increase our faithful behavior because we all walked the right path of faith as children.

We will learn a lot about faith by discussing the relationships we had as children, but we also want to break down the keys of faith we gain in the relationships we choose to start later in life, including ones with our friends and our spouses. All of our relationships in life hold keys to unlocking more faith, but understanding how we used, or are using, our faith in those relationships is how we will open our hearts and minds to exhibit faithful behavior to follow God's will in our lives today.

We already exhibit faith in the relationships that surround our lives. The ultimate goal of our faith is to choose God first and put our relationship with Jesus above all others in our lives. We are about to discuss the numerous ways we should exhibit faith in God in the same ways we do in our relationships with others. Each one of those similarities are keys we can carry with us to find faith in God and use it to follow His path for our lives.

I want to preface that each family and relationship is different. The relationships we are about to discuss may not look exactly like the ones we grew up in. People grow up in many different situations, and with different people surrounding them. When we begin to read these sections, we should picture our relationship with that particular person or people. It is okay if we don't, or didn't, have one or more of the relationships on this list. We can replace that relationship with someone who was a surrogate of that role for us. We may also benefit from reading through each relationship, even if it doesn't pertain to us, so that we can equip ourselves with the knowledge of what type of faith builder God designed that relationship to be.

Father– A description of good father should include that he is a provider, a strong capable working man, and someone we can count on to get things done. A father is someone whom we want in our corner, defending us at all times. A father shows compassion, but is also stern in his corrections. He is the leader of the house, and he is also the leader of the family.

Mother– Our mother is our shelter. She takes care of us. A good mother is affectionate and giving without thought. She is our supporter and our shield. She pushes us to stay motivated and allows room for us to find our path. A good mother often puts the needs of her child in front of her own.

Siblings– Brothers and sisters are the first peer relationships most of us build. They are generally caring and supportive, but not in the way a parent would be. Siblings build our confidence and with them around, we feel safe, secure, and free to be ourselves. Siblings bring out a competitive nature that may allow us to work harder in order to try and garner attention. Brothers and sisters are our first friends, but they can also be our worst enemies, or our biggest fans.

Friends– Friends are the blocks we build around a foundation of family. God gave us friends so that we would have people to share life with. With our friends we will share stories, share laughs, share adventures, share living spaces, and share time together. Friends should be trustworthy because they know our strengths and our weaknesses. Friends are an essential part of any life and have the hands we will often hold to get through it.

Spouse– A good husband or wife is honest. Our spouse needs to be the most honest person in our lives because we chose them to lean on, encourage us, and to stand next to us in battle, and we don't want to fight against the enemy with someone that will lie to us. Our spouse is there to provide our lives with perspective, as an ally and a friend. The role of good spouse should be to serve the other. God says a spouse is a reward from Him. Whoever finds a spouse finds a good thing, and obtains favor from the Lord (Eccles. 9:9, Prov. 18:22).

Now, we have a basic concept of what these relationships should be, so let's examine them further to highlight how each relationship helps us to build our faith in God. These deeper looks will show how our different relationships can ultimately help us better understand God's relationship with us.

Keys from Our Father

"See how very much our Father loves us, for he calls us his children, and that is what we are! But the people who belong to this world don't recognize that we are God's children because they don't know him." **1 John 3:1 (NLT)**

The relationship with our father is designed to be the most important, and faith building, relationship in our lives. A loving father is both nurturing and rewarding. God designed a father to act this way, yet we know not every earthly father is like that. We know not every father sticks around, not every father raises their children in love, and not every father survives. My father passed away when I was twelve years old, so I know about the struggles and grace needed to overcome a life without a dad.

The purpose of a relationship with a loving father is to reflect the relationship we should have with God. 1 John 3:1 tells us that God loves us, sees us *all* as His children, and that the world will have a hard time understanding God because they don't know Him. God gave us earthly fathers we would need to learn to be reliant upon, so that our faith would be able to rely on God when we are older.

The best way to understand how our complete faith in God is possible as adults is to compare it to how children will faithfully rely on their earthly father for all of their needs without worry. A small child doesn't work, cook, or clean. A child doesn't worry about the bills, what's for dinner, or where they should live. Unlike adults, children can put their *entire* faith in their father to provide for them.

God wants us to rely on Him exactly as children would their earthly father because 1 John 3:1 tells us that we are His children, and He is our father.

Faith to rely on a provider has been active inside of us since we were a child. That same faith, once used for our earthly father, will need to be pointed in the direction of our Lord, in order to see Him act as the provider in our lives today.

Testimony

After I quit my paycheck job to go into ministry, it was met with great skepticism by many people in my life, and someone once told me, "God doesn't pay rent!"

A worldly faith believes that since God doesn't sign the check, it must not be God who paid it, but I found out the opposite to be true. After I left my worldly job, I found out that not only does God does pay the rent, but He also pays the rest of the bills, and even provides enough for me to give to others as well. The difference was God didn't always do those things in a conventional way, and many people still believe the way I live my life isn't the right way to do it.

I now have years of evidence to support the claim that relying on God as an adult, with the same faith I did for my father as a child, results in the findings that my heavenly father is my provider.

When we find faith in the relationships we have with our father on earth, and our heavenly father, those relationships will share many similarities. The similarities between both relationships are going to be our keys to faith from our father. When we understand those similarities, we will become equipped to use what we learned from our earthly father to increase our faith in God.

Keys to Faith from Our Father

- **He Wants Us to Live Without Worry**
- **He Corrects Us**
- **He Has a Job for Us to Do**
- **He Loves Us, No Matter What**
- **He Wants to Bless Us**

He Wants Us to Live Without Worry

Our lives will become peaceful when our faith is working properly. We have that peaceful life as children because we rely on our earthly father to provide for us. When we don't transfer that faith over to our heavenly father, worry and doubt will replace peace in our life. When we have a childlike reliance on God to support us, life will be just like a child's—care free and full of joy. Only faith can provide that level of childlike peace.

Children know, or have faith, dad will go to work and provide for them. Children do not fear their father won't keep a roof over their heads, and mature faith in the Lord will respond the same way. A person who lets God be their father will have faith God is working to make sure their life will be provided with the opportunities, resources, and talents it needs to be successful. A person who has faith in the Lord will not worry about losing the roof over their head or about being able to get food on the table. Living without worry is a key to knowing our faith in God is working.

He Corrects Us

Being corrected because we did something wrong in the eyes of our father isn't the best feeling in the world. Seeing disappointment in our father's eyes is heartbreaking. Depending on the situation, he might yell, scream, or avoid us completely. Our faith works in this situation because we know that our father is trying to help improve us by correcting our bad behavior.

As children we don't want to be told what we are doing is wrong, and we definitely do not want to be punished. However, our faith allows us to believe father knows best, and his correction of our bad behavior teaches us what we did was wrong, so we can change bad behavior into good. As adults we continue bad behavior, but there is no longer someone around to correct us, and so, we forget that we need correction. Our faith needs to shift from not wanting to be corrected to actively pursuing correction from the Lord.

As children, we struggle with correction, but we have faith to believe our earthly father knows best. As adults, we may look back and disagree with some of the things our fathers did to correct us. We need to remember that it is true that our earthly father may handle a problem with us incorrectly sometimes, but our heavenly father will never do that. Our key to faith is to know, that when we do something wrong, our heavenly father is there to remind us what we did was a mistake, in the hopes that we will make better decisions in the future. Allowing God to correct our mistakes will make us humble, mature us, and give us wisdom. God wants a loving relationship with us, regardless of our mistakes, just like a good earthly father does.

He Has a Job for Us to Do

As children we are sometimes given chores to do. We take out the trash, mow the yard, or clean up our room. Sometimes, we receive an allowance for doing our chores, and other times we are expected to do them without reward. There are some children who enjoy doing what they are told constantly, and other children who fight every single time they are asked to do something. In the home of a good earthly father we have a job to do in our family, not everyone has the same tasks, but no one goes without one.

For this key to faith to work, we need to perform the tasks God gives us to do for the Kingdom of Heaven, just like we do chores around our house. Both of these tasks are given to us by a father. God has a specific job for us *all* to do, and He has also given us the talents to accomplish them. If we are unsure what our specific task is for the Kingdom of Heaven right now we should lean on God's Word, which says, we should be a blessing to world, help one another, and bear each other's burdens (Gal. 6:2, Mark 12:31).

When trying to find faith to accomplish God given tasks, remember, not everyone has the same task, but they all work together for the kingdom. Sometimes, God expects us to do things that we will eventually be rewarded for. In the same way, we did things for our earthly father and were rewarded with things like an allowance. Our earthly father might have used the phrase "because I said so," when he wanted us to do something that brought no reward. However, sometimes God expects us to do things simply because He asks us to and we should follow His instructions.

Our key to faith is to stay mindful that our relationship with our Lord will develop, as we complete tasks He needs us to accomplish. We learn this key to faithful behavior from following instructions from our father on earth.

He Loves Us, No Matter What

Visit a memory where you did something wrong, and you had to tell your dad. Picture the disappointment or the anger your father may have been feeling towards you after you told him what you did.

Now, picture you had dinner that same night. While you are all gathered around the dinner table, no one is talking. You begin to eat your food, and all of a sudden, you begin to choke. Who jumps up to help? Your father jumps up to your rescue. Why? Isn't he mad at you? Wasn't he angry and yelling at you earlier? Why would he help you if he were so upset? A loving father helps you no matter what you did wrong. The desire of a loving father is to protect, help, and care for you.

In times of trouble, our God comes immediately when we need Him to because He loves us, no matter what. Our faith should be strong in the Lord because we know that He will be the first one to jump up when we are in trouble. Our heavenly father created us, and even in times of strain in our relationship, God wants us to be safe. There is nothing we can do to stop our Lord from loving us.

He Wants to Bless Us

A loving father also wants us to bless us with things we can't get for ourselves. God, as our loving father, has everything we need, and to receive it all we need to do is ask. However, sometimes when we ask, our heavenly father might say, "I don't think you need that right now," just like our earthly father might. We don't always need what we want, and a loving father, just like God, determines when we are in need of something.

> *"You parents—if your children ask for a loaf of bread, do you give them a stone instead? Or if they ask for a fish, do you give them a snake? Of course not! So if you sinful people know how to give good gifts to your children, how much more will your heavenly Father give good gifts to those who ask him."* **Matthew 7:9–11 (NLT)**

The Bible clearly tells us that parents should want their children to ask for their needs to be met and also for good gifts, so they can provide those things to their children. Parents won't respond to the request from their children by blessing them with something that would not fulfill their request. This verse says our heavenly father will do even more to bless us with our requests when we ask Him.

When we ask, and they *do* see our need, our loving father will go out of his way to help us receive whatever it is. A loving father will stay up late helping with a project, drive across the city, and will work extra hours to support his children. He goes that extra mile because a father's love is fulfilled by the happiness of His children. Having this key to faith in God will open doors to our needs, and we learn how to use this key when we ask our father on earth for things. We may not always get what we ask for, but a loving father gets their children what they need when we have faith to ask for it.

How do we carry all these keys with us?

The knowledge we learned to use from the keys of faith from our relationship with our father on earth is meant to inspire our faith in God. The relationship with our earthly father allows us to know, to trust, and to have faith our needs will be met by our heavenly father. We need to let God continually show up for us, just like a loving father does. We need to do it so often we just begin to expect God will provide our lives with blessings just because He loves us, no matter what.

We are now starting to understand that faith has been inside us since we were born. God just wants us to continue to exercise, use, and grow that same faith. We need to get used to letting God take care of us. We need to strengthen our faith, so that we don't even realize we're using it. There was a time we knew Dad would take care of things for us. Instead of changing our faith to think we have to take care of everything ourselves, we need to focus our faith on our heavenly father, who calls us His children, and know God will take care of things.

Keys from Our Mother

"I remember your genuine faith, for you share the faith that first filled your grandmother Lois and your mother, Eunice. And I know that same faith continues strong in you." **2 Timothy 1:5 (NLT)**

While our father is meant to be our provider, our mother is meant to be our caregiver. God designed the role of a loving mother to be comforting, giving, instructing, and caring. A loving mother desires us to live a joyful life that stands apart from others.

Scripture tells us in 2 Timothy 1:5 that our faith can be influenced by the faith of those around us. This was written to Timothy by the apostle Paul in response to a crisis of faith that Timothy was dealing with. Timothy, who would later become a martyr for Christ, was experiencing what many Christians still go through to this day—which is to think, "Is what I'm doing right? Is my faith strong enough? Am I the person who should be doing this?"

Paul used part of his letter to encourage Timothy's relationship with Christ. Paul wrote that it was easy for him to see Timothy's faith, even if Timothy was having a hard time believing he was walking in it. Paul reassures Timothy by telling him that faith is influenced by those around us, and if Timothy was raised by great women of faith, then that great faith was continuing in him.

Since we will spend so much time with our mothers while they care for us as children, our relationships with them will often have the most influence on faith in our lives. Our mothers supply our lives with a number of things as children, and many of those things share qualities with how we will use our faith in our relationship with God. Those qualities are going to be our keys to faith from our mother, and knowledge of them will open our eyes to our need to rely on God with the same faith we use to rely on mom.

Keys to Faith from Our Mother

- **She Supplies Our Needs**
- **She Wants to Be Appreciated**
- **She Desires to Help Us**
- **She Sees Problems Equally**

She Supplies Our Needs

Trusting, and finding faith, for our mother to care, comfort, and help us through any problem is the easiest faith to find as a child. From the moment we are born they watch over us, hold us, and make sure we are okay. Our mothers are also drawn to our cry and desire to supply us with all of our needs including food, warmth, and comfort. Mothers seem to have supersonic hearing for their children. They can hear things that no one else does, even when they are in another room, or away from the conversation. God is also aware of everything in our lives, and He desires to take care of us by meeting our needs.

> *"Look at the birds. They don't plant or harvest or store food in barns, for your heavenly Father feeds them. And aren't you far more valuable to him than they are?"*
> **Matthew 6:26 (NLT)**

Our key to faith is to allow God to supply all of our needs. Using our faith to lean upon God to meet our needs is the same faith we used to believe our mothers would care for us. If we were once able to rely on another person to supply our needs, is it really harder to believe our God, *who created the very things we need*, to be able to supply them? It is the instinct of a loving mother to give their child everything they need or want. That instinct is inside them because we are made in the image of God, and He has the desire to care about the needs of each of us.

She Wants to Be Appreciated

As a child, it is easier for us to hug and kiss our mother for taking care of us than it is to do when we get older. As we grow older and are more reliant on ourselves, we sometimes begin being less appreciative of all the things that our mothers do for us. This is the same way we act with God. Early in our relationship with God, we will constantly praise and thank Him for all He does for us, but as the years pass, we sometimes forget to be as thankful to God as we once were.

A mother's love is supported by their child's reliance on them. A loving mother functions best when she feels needed. A loving mother cannot be what she was intended to be, if we push her away, and don't let her care for us. In that same way, God can't be the caregiver He is meant to be for us when we ignore Him or push Him away.

> *"And whatever you do or say, do it as a representative of the Lord Jesus, giving thanks through him to God the Father."* **Colossians 3:17 (NLT)**

Our key to faith is to recognize that we *need* to be thankful for all God does in our life, in the same way we bless our mother with hugs, kisses, and appreciation as children. The Bible asks us to thank God in everything we say or do. The Bible also says that God inhabits praise, and we all *need* God to inhabit our lives (Ps. 22:3).

Giving thanks to our mother, and God, allows them to know we appreciate all they do in our lives. That appreciation is not necessary because they would care for us without one thank you; however, it is a desire of both our mother and God to be wanted. When we expect a good result and receive one, we are thankful. The definition of faith is expecting a good result and receiving it. That means being thankful to God takes faith!

She Desires to Help Us

God and our mother desire to help us make the best of our lives. However, both relationships understand the need for us to have room to make our own decisions. God and our mother do not want us to get picked on, perform badly in class, or fail at anything, yet they don't *always* step in there when things aren't going our way. They know that life is strengthened through experience, but it doesn't mean they aren't hurt when we don't include them.

We often think we know best, and we often face situations alone because we believe we don't need any help. The longer we rely on our own efforts to face situations the more we often struggle. Relying on others is evidence of being strong in faith. When we try and face life without their help, we will have a much harder time finding that victory. Our key to faith in God is for us to let Him help us find success by sharing our problems with Him, instead of, trying to always figure everything out for ourselves. Our faith should be willing to receive help, and we gain that level of faith as children, when we allow our mothers to help guide us through tough moments in life.

Testimony

I remember a time when I was in middle school, and I had been really struggling with understanding some of my math homework. Several times my mom came into my room and tried to offer assistance with the problems I was having. I refused her help because I felt like I knew more than her about it, and she couldn't possibly understand it.

As I worked by myself, I continued to struggle and was getting extremely frustrated. When she offered her help again later, I lashed out at her. I yelled something like, "Mom, I just don't need your help; you can't help me!" She left the room, and I heard her begin to cry. She was so upset that she told my father all about what had happened when he came home. My father then scolded me for the way I spoke to my mother.

I wasn't able to understand why it was such a big deal. I mean, I just wanted to do it my way! How come that was so wrong; why wasn't that ok?

It took me a long time to understand what actually happened, even though the problem was obvious to my mother. She knew that I was struggling. She knew I was going to continue to struggle, until I let someone come, and help me.

My loving mother exhibited her God-given desire to run to me anytime I was in need. When I pushed her away by telling her she wasn't needed, she was then unable to care for me. She was unable to show her love for me by letting me rely on her. I was, in a sense, unintentionally telling her I didn't care for her love, that it was meaningless to me at that moment, and that my way was better. It wasn't.

Later that night, after the storm of emotions had settled, she came into my room to talk with me, and as she approached me, she spoke with a very loving and caring tone. My mom again asked me if she could help me. This time I knew I couldn't say no anymore. She read through the assignment and then helped me understand it. My mother helped me through my problem, even though I had believed she couldn't.

My mom was a great help to me when I needed it most. Before bed we had a chance to talk about everything that had happened. We both cried about the way we handled the situation, and even though it was a tough moment for us, it brought us closer together.

We feel close to, loved, and nurtured by our mothers because we have faith that they will always be there to help us. That closeness is the same desire our heavenly father has for us. God is constantly waiting for us to go to Him and ask for help. God loves us and knows our needs, but He will let us carve our own path, until we seek Him. When the emotions of our problems subside, God is there to speak to us in a loving and caring tone. God will then guide us through situations we once thought He couldn't.

She Sees Problems Equally

God ultimately wants to help us find solutions to our problems. The size of our problems makes no difference to God, just like loving mothers, because they both want to make our lives better regardless of what the situation is. I know this because my mom shed as many tears that day over math homework, as she did the day I confessed my gambling addiction, but in both situations she had a deep desire to help me in any way she could.

When God sees us struggling, He will always want to jump in there and help us because He sees problems equally. However, we sometimes think our small problems don't need assistance. We don't call mom every time the faucet leaks, the phone bill's late, or our homework is too hard. We have an even harder time bringing small things to God because we think God has better things to do than worry about our daily life. This is not true. God loves us and desires a deep relationship with us (John 15:9-17).

Our key to faith is to recognize that our problems are equal to the Lord and to invite Him into all aspects of our lives.

We need to stop going to God only when tragedy strikes or when we've tried everything, and just can't figure out how to solve our problems on our own. We need to go to God first in all things. We build our faith in this through our mothers as children, by concerning them with everything. We ask them for help tying our shoes, going to the bathroom, and getting dressed. Letting our mothers be involved in every part of our life early on helped train our faith for its need to rely on God for *everything* later on in life.

How do we carry these keys with us?

The faith we learn to use from our relationship with our mother is reliance. We learn to carry that type of faith because we learned to rely on our loving mother throughout life. If we were sick and at the hospital, we just *know* mom will be the first one there. If we called mom after we got bad news, we *know* she will be the one to help us get through any problem. When we are feeling down and just want someone to tell us it will get better, we *know* our mom will tell us that. All of that faith is built up because we have been relying on our mother for so long, and we just *know* she'll be there for us.

What we are exercising when you *know* something, even though it hasn't happened yet, is faith. Faith is when you just *know*, and God wants us to put that same faith in Him so when we are broken hearted we will turn to Him. When God, like our loving mother, tells us everything is going to be all right, we should *know* it will be.

We carry that reliance by letting Christ pick us up when we fall, by calling out to Him when we are troubled and when we let Him supply our needs by asking for help. Trying to navigate this world alone is a daunting task, but that is what we are doing when we leave God out of our problems. A loving mother always seems to know what to say when we are in trouble, and God is no different. God has answers to all life's problems, but we need to carry our keys of faith to unlock His solutions.

Keys from Our Siblings

"Two people are better off than one, for they can help each other succeed." **Ecclesiastes 4:9 (NLT)**

Ecclesiastes 4:9 is clear to tell us that going through life with someone beside us will always be better. God designed our lives to interact. We interact with our families, friends, and God. The Bible tells us when we spend life alone we will make bad decisions for ourselves and begin to seek out our own will for our lives instead of God's (Prov. 18:1).

God's Word in Ecclesiastes tells us that victory, or success, is possible when we have faith in someone besides ourselves. This verse is most commonly used to describe the relationship between a man and a wife, but we will all live several years before reaching that season of life. In our early years, our siblings love for us will be critical for us to find success in many areas of life.

Siblings are our first friends, and the people we will share our lives with growing up. We share playtime, bedrooms, toys, and clothes with siblings, although sometimes not willingly. Since we are so intertwined in our sibling's lives we feel a closeness to them we simply don't share with others. Siblings become our sounding boards, our confidants, and the first brutally honest people we have to deal with in life. Loving siblings will also be the ones who surround us and make us feel safe in troubled times.

The keys to faith we learn from our siblings will help us create an attitude of victory in our lives. Those keys are special because they all have to do with stretching out our faith, whereas we learned to have a foundation of faith in God through our parents. We will use the faith we learn from our siblings when we make big leaps of faith for God later in life. These keys will help fine tune our faith, and see our relationship with God reach a forward-looking level.

Keys to Faith from Siblings

- **They Stretch Us to Reach Further**
- **They Provide Examples**

They Stretch Us to Reach Further

Loving siblings will give one of these two types of opinions when you go to them for advice.

1) They will try and give us wisdom to improve our decisions.
2) They will lead us to make a choice that isn't the wisest, in order to see what happens.

Loving siblings may seem mean spirited when they go with option number two, but this type of behavior is very helpful and does a number of positive things to our lives. Plus, loving siblings won't usually let us do something too wrong without voicing concern.

Siblings aren't as protective as a parent might be, and that space will allow us the opportunity to safely test our limits and opinions when mom and dad aren't around. That freedom results in learning the positive or negative outcome that might follow a particular choice. Faith is all about believing we can find victory in something we are unsure about. We learn that key to faith in God when our siblings stretch us out by getting us to do things out of our comfort zone.

Loving siblings understand that when we make decisions we will either fail or succeed, but either way, we tried. A loving sibling knows we can't find success without trying, and they will always be encouraging us out of our comfort zone. A parent might nudge us to avoid a cliff; however, a sibling might nudge us over its edge.

Siblings aren't as concerned with the failure aspect of our lives like a parent might be because they know we are resilient. They ultimately know that pushing us towards action will make us better.

As we walk with Christ, we will encounter many opportunities to step out in faith. When God wants us to do something for Him, it may sound a lot like when a sibling tried to get us to do something crazy that we are unsure about. God, wants us to trust Him, and uses those seemingly foolish opportunities to stretch our faith to do His will and prove that His plan is better.

Jesus asked Peter to step of a boat, a man to wash his eyes in a pool to receive sight, and asked the apostles to go and share the gospel with all of creation (Matt. 14:28; John 9:7; Acts 1:8). Each time Jesus asked them to do things that were out of their comfort zone. Jesus wants us to take big leaps of faith to find big victory for the Kingdom of Heaven. The key to our faith in God that allows us to stretch out towards things we are unsure we will reach is learned through our relationships with our siblings.

They Provide Examples

Faith sometimes writes itself onto our hearts by the actions we see others take. Watching others step out in faith increases our own desire to step out in faith. Our siblings are our first consistent example of this behavior that we see. They forge a path ahead for us to see, that allows us to make better decisions for ourselves when facing similar situations, because we can decide to follow behind them or make our own new path to try and find better results.

Most of us have heard people tell stories about how they were inspired or influenced by their siblings. We hear testimonies of how proud they are of their siblings because they were the first ones that went to college or because they picked up the slack from working, or missing, parents. We have heard the story about a younger sibling who found strength to push harder and achieved more because they wanted to stand out. These stories inspire our faith by example.

God wants our faith in Him to be encouraged by these types of stories (Rev. 12:11). Our siblings are the first ones to encourage our faith by action because they are our peers, and we *know* if they can do something, we can to. God wants us to understand early on that our testimonies are written by our actions, and watching someone take risks, try hard, and overcome a tough past to find success will inspire us to do those same things. God wants us to put our faith in action inside His will for our lives so that we can find irrefutable success through Christ.

How do we carry these keys with us?

Loving siblings influence our life and help build our faith. Siblings teach us acceptance, structure and the balance that our life needs to be productive and faith filled. We carry the keys of faith we learn from them by maintaining a desire to do what God has called us to do with our lives. When we are focused on our future that Jesus died to bring us we are in faith. The future plans God has for our lives will often include trying, and learning new things. Trying new things may not be comfortable or seem so easy, but when we take those big steps towards Jesus, God has a plan for our faith to pay off in a big way.

The testimony our life creates from taking big leaps of faith for God needs to be shared with others. Sharing our stories about how we found success when we stepped off our own boats will inspire the faith for Christ in others, and encourage us to step off the boat faster next time. Choosing to follow God's will for our lives, and sharing our personal testimonies of victory along that path with others, will also show that a relationship with Jesus Christ as Lord and Savior provides the best possible ending for our future.

Key from Our Friends

"As iron sharpens iron, so a friend sharpens a friend."
Proverbs 27:17 (NLT)

Proverbs 27:17 paints a picture of iron sharpening iron to illustrate how friendship works. When iron sharpens iron it creates both friction and sparks. Friendship does the same thing, but that doesn't mean it is a bad result. When iron sharpens irons, it produces something that is stronger, sharper, and more useful than before. When friends sharpen each other, they produce similar results, and become better versions of the people we were before. Friendships strengthen our foundation, sharpen our minds, and make us more useful to the world by shaping us into maturity.

Even though friendships sometimes come with friction and sparks, they more often come with support and love. Loving friends have their own distinct role and purpose for building our faith in God. There is one major key to faith in God that our relationships with our friends unlock. This key is a building block to realizing that God loves us no matter what. This key reminds us that nothing we ever do can stop Him from loving us, His strength covers our weaknesses, and His grace covers all our sin (2 Cor. 12:9).

Key to Faith from Our Friends

- **Acceptance**

Acceptance

Our friends accept us. Loving friends won't leave our lives because of what we do for a living, where we grew up, went to school, or who we choose to be in a relationship with. Friends will usually protect our name from being dragged through the mud, even if those things are true. Loving friends are also very proud of us and are happy to tell everyone they know about our accomplishments.

If we can have faith that our friends will accept us no matter what, we should be using that faith to let the Lord accept us no matter what.

Acceptance is what brings our relationships with our friends, and Jesus, close together. Friends just understand each other, and Jesus is our friend (John 15:15). Friends know all of our secrets, and all of our successes. Jesus does too, and the unconditional acceptance He provides brings a level of trust we may not have with any of our family or friends.

How does acceptance produce faith? Acceptance provides faith because no matter what happens, or where life takes us, our loving friends aren't going anywhere. In fact, the bumpier the ride gets the closer they usually get (Prov. 18:24). That same idea applies to how our faith should be accepting of whatever situation God has for us. The bumpier the life, the closer we need to get to God. Our faith in God, just like our friendships, should get stronger and not farther away from us when trouble comes.

Testimony

There was this man who worked at a fish market with his family. He went to start a new job as a teacher. This decision was not well received within everyone in his family. Some were very supportive, and some decided it was an unforgivable offense, and hardly spoke to this man again. This man held closely to his friends during this time, and they became his new family.

One friend stood out among the others. The two shared everything together, and as the man continued to go through tough times transitioning to his new job, his friend continued to encourage and explain to him that he was doing the right thing, even though it didn't look like it to everyone else. His friend listened to him when he was struggling, offering advice and consolation.

This man sometimes wasn't sure if he was meant to be a teacher. He thought that maybe it would be easier to go back to the routine of his old life and do what he was comfortable doing. His friend accepted him how he was, with all of his doubts and successes. Thanks to that encouragement the man stayed at his new job and became a great teacher, and he credits all the success he had at that new job to his friend.

This is the testimony of Peter, who left his job, and family business, as a fisherman in order to take the job Jesus offered Him to become an apostle. It must've been tough for Peter, who was expected to take over his father's fishing company, to stay faithful during moments that his family and others around him criticized his decision to take a job as an apostle.

During the times Peter struggled in his new job, Jesus stood close to him. Jesus loved and accepted Peter regardless of his lack of faith, his poor decisions, or his behavior (Matt. 8:26, 26:75; John 18:10, 21:15-19). Peter trusted and had faith in his friend Jesus, just like we are supposed to. Jesus will, in turn, love, and accept us as a friend, regardless of our doubt, sin, or behavior (Rom. 15:7).

Our faith in God can be built up and made stronger by understanding our relationship with our own loving friends. Friends accept us no matter where we are going in life. Loving friends should, however, encourage us to go farther, do more, and accomplish our goals. Peter's life, just like ours, wasn't always easier because he followed Christ. Jesus, like our loving friends, helped pick him up, and built his faith by accepting him in his struggle. Our lives today are filled with constant turbulence and problems, and our friends who love us, will be there to help us find victory in those times. Jesus said He would never leave us (Heb. 13:5). Don't we all want a best friend like that?

How will we carry this key to faith with us?

We carry this key of acceptance by reminding ourselves daily that Jesus is our friend, He isn't going anywhere, and He wants us to succeed. We need to remember Jesus won't forsake us regardless of what seas are raging against our boat. Having faith in Christ to be accepted how we are may be difficult, but knowing that we have already displayed that type of faith in our friendships allows us to know it isn't impossible.

We can probably think of at least one or two people in our lives that will always be there for us. Our faith is in those friends to do anything for us, protect our best interests, be proud of us, and want to be near us. We will trust a loving friend to show up to help when we move and to be there when we invite them out, as much as we will expect them to show up for all of our major life events. We should trust, and expect, God to be in our lives like that as well!

Jesus wants to be our friend (John 15:15). Our friendship with Jesus needs to be just as much a part of our life as those who are on our phone contact list. When we call Jesus, He will always answer our call, and be there in our lives to encourage, help, and console us. Carrying our key of faith in God to be accepted by Him is as simple as putting Jesus on our friend list. Jesus has already accepted our friend request and all we have to do is start treating Him like one. We need to keep Christ informed about what we are up to all the time and expect Him to be there for us when need Him.

Key from Our Spouse

"He who finds a wife finds a good thing and obtains favor from the Lord." **Proverbs 18:22 (ESV)**

One of the greatest gifts God gives His people is the opportunity to find their spouse and get married. Proverbs 18:22 says that a spouse is a good thing. A spouse is our lover, leader, provider, manager, and supporter. A loving spouse is in it good or bad, tough or easy, healthy or sick, until death ends the marriage.

Since a spouse is one of the greatest gifts God gives, it is also one of the greatest areas of attack by the enemy. The enemy kills, steals, and destroys what is most precious to God, and marriage is precious to God. God's idea for marriage and the joy that comes with it is precious because it is a reflection of His deep love for us.

The key to faith in God we gain from a loving spouse is a representation of God's overflowing love for us. God loves us deeply and shows us that love with His actions, and a loving spouse does the same thing. The faith we learn from our spouse allows us to understand the relationship dynamic between God and ourselves. When we begin to use this key to faith we will have a deep understanding of God's love for us, because this key can only be used when we put someone's desires above our own. Jesus gave us the ultimate example of using this key and putting everyone first when He came to Earth as a man and became a servant of *all*.

Key to Faith from Our Spouse

- Giving

Giving

God loved so much He gave (John 3:16). Giving is how the Bible illustrates love and how God wants us to express it. *Giving* is God's definition of love. Love is *not* just a feeling. Feelings come and go, and change based on circumstances. Love, as defined by God, is to put the needs above others first regardless of the circumstances. Learning and understanding God's definition of love is crucial for the success of any marriage.

Jesus love for us took Him to the cross to die for our sins. The beating, torture, and disrespect Christ had to endure for that love is not something He did just because he felt like it.

The faith Jesus used to *give* His life at the cross is evidence of how much He loves us. The love we have for our spouse should reflect the same love Jesus had for all of us.

> *"For husbands, this means love your wives, just as Christ loved the church. He gave up his life for her."* **Ephesians 5:25 (NLT)**

When we get married, we are giving up our former life to create a new life. Our spouses' joys, dreams, and choices are now connected to ours. That is why God tells us we become one flesh. Losing our old life is not a bad thing, even though it may sound like it. Instead, we are gaining the opportunity to share one life with someone else, and God says sharing our life leads to success (Eccles. 4:9).

Learning to have faith to love God and give our lives to Him like Jesus did is very difficult because we are all born into sin. Since we were born selfish because of sin, the idea of putting the needs or wants of someone else first isn't always easy to do. We spend all our lives with our own needs to think about, and changing that behavior needs training. God was aware of the struggle we were going to face, so He created marriage as a training ground for having the faith to give our lives to serve the Kingdom of Heaven.

When we give something away there is a fear. When we give our heart away, we might be afraid it will get broken. When we give our money away, we are afraid we won't have enough for later. When we give our children away to marriage, we're afraid we won't be needed anymore. The key to faith in God is to remove all of that fear and replace it with hope.

If we are a great spouse that does everything we can to be loving, caring and affectionate, it is because we do it with the heart or the desire to do it and not just because we think we have to. When we act in faith, by giving them that behavior, we aren't usually fearful that they won't return that same love or affection back on us. When we love our spouse, we love without a net because we have faith our love to give won't cause us to fall.

When we give to our spouse, we don't expect anything in return. A loving spouse will do things simply out of love and not out of obligation. God loves us in this same way. God's grace by definition is an unrequited gift, which is a gift the giver doesn't expect to be paid back for. God gives His grace out of love, the same way we give someone a birthday present.

Do we give someone a birthday present based solely on whether or not they were going to get us one, or do we give someone a birthday present as an act to show our love for them? We give to show our love, and that is how God's grace and love work in our life. Grace is given by God without measure, and without fear that we won't appreciate it. Grace is designed to show us how to love.

Think about the joy you feel when you watch someone open the present *you* got for them. You aren't interested as much when they open other presents, but when they get to your gift, you become excited. You become hopeful that they are overjoyed with it, and you want them to be happy they received it because knowing that will also make you happy.

Giving isn't something we should be afraid of to do because of the possible consequences. God showed us, through all His actions, that giving is the greatest way to show love. God wants to bless us and see our faces light up in happiness. God wants to see the look on our faces when we realize how perfect it is. Salvation, new life, new purpose, hope, foundation, joy, peace, kindness, and gentleness are just some of the gifts He has to give us, and God wants us to open them all.

We learn the most about giving through our spouse. Marriage provides the best lesson we can learn about God's giving love for us because it gives us the opportunity to mirror that behavior towards our spouse. We sometimes think we give more to our children than our spouses; however, a loving marriage will often outlast the time a child stays at home. We will spend more time with our spouse than we ever will with our children. That time will be spent serving one another, and all those opportunities will be the classroom we use to learn how to give faithfully.

How will we carry this key to faith with us?

Marriage is important to God. The Bible illustrates this importance by calling believers the bride of Christ (2 Cor. 11:2). As our spouse, Jesus wants to give us everything He has and make us a part of His life. In return, Christ also wants us to choose to lay down our lives and follow Him (Mark 8:34–38). God gives us marriage on Earth to prepare us for the sacrifice of our life for someone else.

We carry this key to faith when we begin to choose to define our lives by how we give. Showing our family, friends, and God our love by giving up our desires to serve them will not always be easy and it will take daily sacrifice of our time, energy, and resources. To truly follow Christ we will also need to give those things to people we don't know, don't want to help, and don't like.

> *"Such love has no fear, because perfect love expels all fear. If we are afraid, it is for fear of punishment, and this shows that we have not fully experienced his perfect love."*
> **1 John 4:18 (NLT)**

Finding faith in God includes giving away our desires to see the desire of others met first. Our sin nature will make us fear that when we give too much of ourselves away we will be punished in some way. We must rid ourselves of the fear caused by our sin nature to exhibit the perfect love of God – which is to give. We should not worry to lose what we give because God says our giving is blessed (Luke 6:38). God also says we should not fear we will be without because He will take care of our needs (Matt. 10:31). When we find our faith secure in God we will be able to give everything we can to see His abundant plan fulfilled through our lives.

Part Three:
How Faith Affects Our Lives

Faith Creates Our Behavior

"But let him ask in faith, with no doubting, for the one who doubts is like a wave of the sea that is driven and tossed by the wind. For that person must not suppose that he will receive anything from the Lord; he is a double-minded man, unstable in all his ways." **James 1:6–8 (ESV)**

Our level of faith isn't always the same. Some days we walk through life with a great expectation for God to show up in our lives, and other times we find ourselves wondering if God is ever going to show up at all. Our faith fluctuates based on our circumstances because the enemy uses our trials to persuade us into believing that God will, indeed, not show up. Our goal should be to never waver in our faith in God, no matter what trial we may be facing because God is always with us (Josh. 1:9).

In this passage of scripture James describes a double-minded man. We all face circumstances that can cause faith, doubt, and indifference to run through our minds. To find faith, we will need to sort through those thoughts, and throw out our doubt and unsureness. James is telling us that double mindedness can cause us to miss out on the Lord's blessings.

James is describing the constantly flowing thoughts of man, comparing them to water being tossed by the wind. James is specific to detail that no thought we have provides stability, except for faith in God. Even though our thoughts are constantly changing, we need to continue to faithfully believe in the Lord to provide our stability, even in uncertainty.

If we are double-minded, that means there will always be multiple thoughts in our mind. When we sort through all those thoughts in our mind and decide what we believe will happen, we will begin to act on our beliefs.

We have three types of believing that lead to our actions. Our actions will *always* fall into one of these groups. Once we see where our thinking is guiding our behavior, we will be better equipped to recognize faith-filled behavior and use it to hold on to our Lord for stability.

Three Types of Believing

- **Doubters**
- **Triers**
- **Believers**

Doubters

Doubters are people who have no faith in anything or anyone. Doubting is reserved for those who don't know what God has for them. Doubters look around and see a life that's already been messed up, and they don't think there is any point in trying to improve their situation.

Doubters don't understand that God promises an abundant life. It is more rational for a doubter to believe they are walking the world aimlessly than it is for them to believe that they have a creator, a designed purpose, and a promise of a better life.

Faith comes by hearing the Word of God, and doubters never hear faith because they never speak words of faith that comes through Christ (Rom. 10:17). Doubters also disregard words of faith when they hear it from others.

Faith is activated by positive words declaring positive outcomes, and then believing they will arrive. Doubters are the people who say things like, "*I'll* never have that," "I wish I could do that with *my* life," or "My life was just *meant* to be this way." This type of thinking will lead to the use of negative words that, when used, will disable faith and prevent all the positive outcomes that faith brings into our life.

When we are in doubt, our mind is cluttered like a garage we can't pull our car into. When our minds are cluttered we have nowhere to park our things like ideas, dreams, or faith for our future. Doubters fill their minds, like a cluttered garage, with useless things they never use. Those useless things, like worry, low self-esteem, and selfish attitude, become valuable to a doubter because they already have them. It's a lot easier for a doubter to keep their negative beliefs in their head, than it is to empty out their mind, and fill it with faith, hopes, and dreams.

God has more for us, but we have to have faith in Him to receive it. No real blessing comes without God and faith activates blessings. When we are in the doubting stage of believing, we need to remember in order to be blessed we need faith to get those blessings moving. When we begin to behave in a manner that is faithful, even in one area of our life, we become a trier.

Triers

This is the category that the beliefs of most people in this world fall into. Triers find it difficult to keep up with the routine of working for change in their life. Triers are those of us that are willing to work on a solution when we see a problem in our lives. However, when triers don't see gratification soon enough they become discouraged. In other words, they realize the cluttered garage is dirty and needs to be cleaned out, but get discouraged when it isn't emptied easily.

Most of the time faith for God's will in our lives will require a lot of patience for us to receive God's blessing. Since triers are people who want more, but have a hard time with patience and perseverance, they have a hard time understanding what's taking so long. In order to see results from their faith faster, a trier will often move their attention to another area of life or try and find a solution to their problem without God. Abraham and Sarah's decision to allow Abraham to have Ishmael with Hagar is a good example of how triers want to see blessings but go looking for their own way when God doesn't provide His blessings immediately.

Triers aren't content with the way their lives are, and they *know* they want something different, but aren't exactly sure how to get it. They constantly search for all sorts of different things to try, so they can find something that provides happiness for them.

Triers often fall short of many goals because they can't stay focused on one thing. God wants us to be diligent in our faith in Him, and a trier will lose interest, and stop travelling down the road of faith towards God because their immediate results aren't what they expected.

Triers might say things like, "I want a new car," "I think I should get a different job," or "I should go back to school." We all know people who say things like this, and many of us have said them ourselves. Triers know there are improvements that need to be made in their lives, and may even begin to look into making changes. However, when triers don't get a car at the first lot they shop at, a job on the first application they turn in, or accepted to the school they want to go to, they may become discouraged to continue to take additional actions to make needed changes to see God's will be done in their lives.

Triers often lack perseverance because when they try to work things out on their own, and without God, they will never actually be working on the right solution. So, even whole hearted attempts will often fall flat because we are lacking the faith in God to see them through, the hope from God to chase after His will, and the grace God gives us to persevere through trials.

Without finding faith to believe for a better future, we are guaranteed to stay where we are in life, and never find the real joy we keep looking for. A trier's nature is to keep doing things their way first, instead of following God, and that behavior will lead to frustration and failure. The good news is that God has a great plan for our life.

God has every area of our life mapped out, and He is ready to share it with us. God's plan for our life will satisfy all our hopes and dreams. We can have that feeling of satisfaction every day, if we move our faith from trying to do it all by ourselves and, instead, give all that faith to God and follow His plan for our life. When we use our faith to persevere through the stage of trying, we enter into faithful believing.

Believers

Being a believer is more than just believing in God, giving our life to Christ, and believing we've been saved. Believing is the type of faith that is talked about in the book of Matthew.

> *"You can enter God's Kingdom only through the narrow gate. The highway to hell is broad, and its gate is wide for the many who choose that way. But the gateway to life is very narrow and the road is difficult, and only a few ever find it."* **Matthew 7:13–14 (NLT)**

True faith is the road less traveled. Taking this path will cause great joy, but also be full of tight turns, obstacles, and valleys to cross. The good news is, when we have believer-sized faith, it means we have given our trust to God to give us a path around, over, and through those problems.

A believer is unlike a trier or a doubter. A believer never wavers in their trust in God's hand over any situation. A believer won't struggle when the garage isn't clear, they will just continue working until it is. A believer won't try to find their own solutions to problems because they know God will show up and provide one. The joyful singing of Paul during his imprisonment described in the book of Acts is a great example of this type of believing. Paul knew God would show up regardless of what the circumstances looked like (Acts 16:25).

A believer is someone who strives for more of God in their lives, and whose beliefs match what God promises them for their future. Believers will never want to stay where they are, although they will be satisfied to stay there while they wait for more of God's will to be revealed so that they can chase after it. It's great to want more, and God *will* give us more (Eph. 3:20). However, God also expects us to be happy while we wait for blessings to arrive because if we truly have faith in God we already believe it has (Ps. 37:7).

Being a believer means we should be just as happy the day we pray for a blessing as we are on the actual day we receive it.

God supplies food, houses, cars, vacations, friends, family, and anything else we could ask or think for. Faith, doesn't always supply those things in the way we think it should because sometimes what we ask for doesn't always line up with God's will. God's plan for the success in our life is not the same success the world believes it should be and sometimes not what we think it should be, either.

We can have joy, with or without a million dollar home, the best looks, or fame. Joy can exist in a life where disease has been diagnosed, or in the lives of those dealing with a handicap. We need to find faith to find joy, and we find faith when we believe the promise of Jesus that where we are going is better than where we are. Believers know that whatever God has for them will be satisfying regardless of how it looks to others. That type of believing brings joy to their life.

We will absolutely stay where we are, and likely get worse, without adding faith for God's will to take place in our life. The good news though is that there are plenty of directions for us to point our faith towards the future. A doubter can't find anything worth doing. A trier can't do anything that requires perseverance. A believer *can* look forward to, work hard for, and find satisfaction in many things, such as eternal life, healing, a family, a spouse, an awesome job, a new home, finding friends, getting an education, or serving others. A believer understands there is so much to look forward to in this life and the next, but it can't get started without faith.

These three types of believing will always be our options. Our minds will sort through our thoughts, and our thoughts determine our actions. Doubters will never find joy while they have doubt because doubt prevents faith from bringing blessings. Triers will always want more out of life but have a hard time finding it. Triers will follow a cycle of losing what they strive for and receiving what they work for. Those two things never match up.

Believers should understand that what God has planned for us is the same thing we should have planned for ourselves. Those two things do match up. God made us, and He gave us our personality, skills, and talents to succeed in our purpose. God doesn't have a life planned out for us that we won't like, even though the world will likely tell us otherwise. If we seek after the life the world tries to tell us to find for ourselves we will end up not feeling satisfied.

A believer will give up the need for control and work hard for God to see faith rewarded. The believing type of faith can't be realized without Christ because we won't be able to gain the knowledge of what God actually wants us to use our faith in Him for until we give all our life to Christ. Our faith will be most effective when we start trying to do the things God calls us to do. Finding faith in God's plan for our lives will bring us complete joy day after day, no matter what that plan is.

Faith Allows Us to Work Hard

"But as for you, be strong and courageous, for your work will be rewarded." **2 Chronicles 15:7 (NLT)**

There is a saying that goes, "The grass is always greener on the other side". This cliché describes people who are interested in having a life they see others have because it must be better than what they have. However, the people on the other side of fence are saying the same thing. So, neither side is actually better off than the other. This is a perfect description of our sinful nature because it will always want something different, and perceivably better, than what we already have, even when it isn't actually better.

How do we know wanting what other people have is a sin? We know because "thou shall not covet" is one of the Ten Commandments. God's commandments are a reminder that we need a savior because we cannot live our lives without breaking them. Coveting is sin we all struggle with, but we often covet without calling it that.

We use credit cards to buy things we can't afford because we want the better life the purchase provides. We borrow things from others all the time because we want what they have. Our lives have been saturated with the idea that we need bigger, faster, and better. Cars, homes, tools, computers, and televisions are just some of the items we want the biggest and best versions of. We want what we want, and we want it now, and that is what covetousness looks like.

We covet because it is easier to get the things we want by using a credit card, stealing, or borrowing, than it is to have faith in God for something to show up through prayer, patience, and hard work.

2 Chronicles 15:7 tells us to be strong and our hard work will be rewarded. Faith is hard work. There is nothing harder than believing for something to come that seems to contradict our circumstances. However, hard work in God's eyes will be rewarded. When we put our trust and faith in Him, as well as our willingness to work for what God promises, we will find a reward for our effort.

The world believes when we work hard, it is our effort that is rewarded. However, for believers it is actually our faith in God's better future that propels us to work hard, and in turn, be rewarded.

> *"So also faith by itself, if it does not have works, is dead. But someone will say, "You have faith and I have works." Show me your faith apart from your works, and I will show you my faith by my works. You believe that God is one; you do well. Even the demons believe—and shudder! Do you want to be shown, you foolish person, that faith apart from works is useless?"* **James 2:17–20 (ESV)**

This scripture is clear to point out the argument between the beliefs of the world, and the way God wants us to believe. James tells us that faith won't put us where we want to go unless hard work follows up that faith. He also writes that hard work is motivated by faith, which means we don't work for things we don't believe will work out. If we are only working for things we believe will work out for the better, it means we only work when we have faith because that behavior is the definition of faith.

If we were told the project we are working on wasn't going to be needed, would we continue to work on it? If we were told we wouldn't pass a test even if we studied, would we still study? If we were told our lives would never get better, would we even get out of bed? No, because our hard work is driven by faith, and we only work hard when we want something to happen. We work hard to pay for the things we want, we study hard because we want better opportunities, and we work hard raising our children right, so they can have a better life than we do. We will not improve our circumstances without faith.

If our faith isn't in something, we really won't try to achieve it. If we don't believe in God, we won't really work to have Him be a part of our life. If we don't believe in a brighter future through God's will for our lives, we won't really do all that we can to follow Him. If we don't believe our situation can improve, we won't really do the hard work to change it, even if that hard work is just saying a prayer in faith.

People often say the grass is greener on the other side, but when we are in faith with God, we will never want to stand on the other side of the green grass because what God has picked out for us is the perfect spot for our lives. Our faith in God allows us to stand in that spot and be blessed by Him.

> *"But blessed are those who trust in the Lord and have made the Lord their hope and confidence. They are like trees planted along a riverbank, with roots that reach deep into the water. Such trees are not bothered by the heat or worried by long months of drought. Their leaves stay green, and they never stop producing fruit."* **Jeremiah 17:7-8 (NLT)**

Testimony

The street I grew up on was a straight road where you would see almost anywhere. However, unlike most streets, there was a court adjacent to my house, and it was sort of out of place. Picture the court as a handle to a briefcase, and my street as the long part attached to the handle.

Growing up, I knew many people who lived on that court. I went over there a lot as a boy and saw that those houses were not in the same condition as mine. I felt like my house was a normal middle class house growing up. I grew up in a clean home, wore nice clothes, ate dinner at the table every night, and took vacations with my family every year.

The houses on the court were not like that. They smelled a little funny when I walked in them. They weren't kept as clean, their garages were often cluttered, and it was normal for them to have cars that didn't run, and yards that were unkempt.

I used to think these people were dirt poor, but I never associated my house with these houses. In other words, I thought my family was better off than most people I knew on the court. Even though we were literally across the street from each other, I felt the street separated us. When I crossed that street as a child, I thought I was going from my life of luxury to go hang out in the slums.

Then one day as an adult, I was having a conversation with my mother. My mother told me how hard she worked to put dinner on the table every night and how she picked up after us all day long. My mom told me our house was clean because she worked tirelessly to keep it that way. Mom told me how long she had to go without, so she could save to take us on a nice vacation every year and also so we could have a great Christmas. My mom told me we were never really as well off as I would often tell her I thought we were.

The revelation finally came to me. We were just like the people in the houses across the street. I had to ask myself why I thought we were so different. My mom wanted us to have a good life, and she made it happen. I thought that everyone wanted to have a good life. The question I kept asking was:

If every family in every house wants a better life, why don't they have it?

Every family doesn't get a better life because they lack faith in God to believe their lives can get better. Without faith they wouldn't really work for what they wanted. To have faith for God's will to be done in our life, we need to expect positive results regardless of our circumstances.

My mom saw us living a more abundant life than what our circumstances allowed others on the same street to see for their lives. My mom had faith in a better life and worked really hard to achieve it for us. I am so thankful for her faith in God and am blessed to have been taught faithful behavior.

There are many people, like those I saw across the street, who found it easier to give up and thought the life they had was as good as was going to get for them. I watched as some of my neighbors stopped worrying about cleaning up the house, they stopped making sure they looked "presentable", and they stopped caring about others.

I also watched as some tried to make attempts to better their lives. They would look for new or better jobs, try and put the house up for sale to get a fresh start somewhere else, or do a massive cleaning of their home inside and out. Most of the time though trying to find a new way wouldn't work out for them how they wanted. The job would be a bust, the house wouldn't sell, or their house would get dirty again because they didn't have the motivation to make cleaning a routine.

I watched as my mom did the opposite of those around me. My mom was a waitress, and while she didn't have the world's most prestigious job, she knew how to work. My mom's tireless work ethic is above and beyond that of anyone else I have ever seen up close. My mom stayed focused and worked hard all the time and she never went without having a job. After my dad died, my mom was unexpectedly on her own and responsible for three kids by herself. Her work had doubled overnight. My mom would leave for work around 4:30 a.m. and spend all day on her feet. My mother would come home, cook dinner for us, clean our rooms, and take us to whatever activity one of us had. My mom would then help us manage whatever life crisis we were going through that week.

My mom has lived her entire life putting the desires of others first. We never felt like we were living in lack because she worked tirelessly, so we didn't have to. Her behavior was set apart from those in the houses around us. Our lives were, in turn, set apart from the lives around us. While we were not well off by worldly standards, I always felt like we had more than everyone else. We had joy because we had faith. I had faith in mom, and she had faith in God's will that our circumstances wouldn't prevent our future from being bright. My mom had faith to work hard.

Faith Produces Our Testimonies

"And they have defeated him by the blood of the Lamb and by their testimony. And they did not love their lives so much that they were afraid to die." **Revelation 12:11 (NLT)**

We all love being the first one to tell someone something. There is no credit given to the person who tells a story second. Reporters make their living on being the one who breaks a story. Punch lines aren't as funny the second time. The person who gives the information first is most often the one who receives the recognition.

When we call someone to share news like, "Did you hear so and so is pregnant," only to hear a less than triumphant, "Yeah, I saw that on Facebook," we will be let down to know we aren't the first ones to share the news. Our happiness is lessened when we aren't the first ones to tell a story, especially good ones, because we want to feel that sense of excitement that comes with eliciting a reaction out of someone. When we share that moment with someone, it tends to satisfy something inside all of us.

These satisfying moments are called our testimonies. Testimonies are often believed to be the story someone tells about the moment they found Jesus; however, our testimony is much more than that. Our testimony includes any story we tell to others. We give a testimony any time we give an account of our life to someone else. When we tell others where we were earlier, things that happened while we were there, or what we are planning for the future, we are telling a part of our testimony.

Our testimony encompasses our entire life, and it is very important to God that we share that testimony, or the story of our lives and faith in Christ, with others.

Revelation 12:11 gives us an important look at the importance of our testimony. A testimony is what we are doing anytime we share news, good or bad, with someone. This verse tells us that telling our story will allow us to overcome the adversity that enemy has put in our lives. Revelation 12:11 says, that the enemy brought sin, but the blood of Jesus overcame it and goes on to say the enemy also brings pain, suffering, and doubt into our lives, and it is our testimonies that allow us overcome those things.

We overcome through our testimony because it is our faith in God's will for our lives that produces our stories of victory. We can't overcome anything without faith. If we have a testimony of victory to tell, it means we had faith to see our circumstances improve. Our faith in Christ produces a testimony that, when told to others, is a powerful witness to God's good work in our lives that led us to victory.

Our faith in God produces our testimony because the stories we tell others are directly linked to our beliefs. When we don't have faith, we share negative stories about how bad we have it. Negative stories are the testimonies of doubters. A trier will share stories about how they tried something, and it didn't work out. A believer, however, will share their testimonies of victory that come from following God's will, even if those victories haven't shown up yet.

Testimonies are meant to be a moment to share our great faith with others, and they were designed by God to encourage whoever hears them to want and believe for more. When we share the results of our faith through our testimonies with someone, we are letting people know we love them because testimonies *give* hope, and love is shown when we give. However, not every testimony we give provides that love because we aren't always sharing our stories of victory. The enemy knows the power of our positive testimony, and he will constantly be trying to put us in a place in life where we feel negative words are needed to describe our situation instead of faithful ones.

There are three different types of testimonies we tell. Our level of faith becomes evident based on which type of testimony we are telling. The faith of the listener will, in turn, be influenced by the stories we tell. Our words have tremendous power and will either increase faith or doubt in those that hear them. Faith to follow God's will comes from hearing the Word of God, so it is important that we speak scripture to stand on and support our beliefs (Rom. 10:17).

We cannot increase faith in others when we share our testimonies about our problems, how we are unsure how to solve them, and our frustrations about them. The job of a believer is to share the testimonies of our good news, as well as our belief in God to solve our problems, so that everyone knows we have been given power to overcome the attacks of the enemy.

Types of Testimonies

- **Our Lack of Success**
- **World's Problems**
- **Success**

Our Lack of Success

Failure is a very common testimony. We will generally tell others how bad things are in our lives or how we've failed at something and just don't understand why. We give testimonies of failure to elicit reactions of sympathy and empathy from the listener. Our hope when we tell stories of failure is that the listeners will want to comfort us, tell us everything will be okay, and tell us that our failures happened for reasons outside of our control.

It's great that we want support for our problems; however, we will never find what we truly need when we look for support from someone other than God. Instead of going to the world to share our failures, we need to first share our testimonies of failure to the ears of God, so that He can give peace and hope for our future. Our testimony of failures, problems, and complaining will never encourage faith in our minds or the minds of others.

Let's look at some common testimonies of failure:

- I can't get a job because no one is hiring.
- I didn't make any money at work today because it was so slow.
- I don't know how I'm going to pay rent this month because people don't tip me more.
- My team lost again because my teammates are so bad.
- My food was bad, and I can't believe they messed up such an easy order.
- My kids suffer because my ex should've done what he/she was supposed to do.
- I have so much homework, and this teacher always gives so much.
- I sat in traffic for an hour, and that's why I was late.

These are common everyday ways of talking for most people. Social media posts have made it easy for us to vent our problems, struggles, and failures to the world in the hopes that people will sympathize and console us for how tough we have it. Even if we aren't the ones sharing failure type testimonies, we are at least hearing or seeing them from someone in our lives. When we constantly see and hear failures from others, it will eventually begin to break down our faith in God's will.

It is in our sin nature to share testimonies of failure. We like to complain by telling others how we are not happy with the way things are going in our lives, but because of our sin nature, we don't often blame ourselves for our problems. The moment we believe victory over a situation is not coming we declare that it's not our fault it didn't come. We will blame someone, or something else, long before we believe it was our own actions that prevented our success. **We are quick to share our stories of victory and take all the credit for how it happened; however, when failure comes, we are not as quick to take credit for the fault.**

Look back at those common testimonies of failure. Each story provides a problem or failure and then lists what caused it. For example, when someone says, "I can't get a job (problem) because no one is hiring (what's to blame for the problem)."

When we tell stories about our lack of success, it is almost always because someone or something prevented our success. We give our lack of success testimonies because we want to hear the words, "Everything will be alright," "that stinks," or "I'm glad that didn't happen to me." Those words provide relief for our minds. Sympathy lets us feel like our problems are bigger than everyone else's, and we find satisfaction in believing everyone has it easier than we do. We like the way we feel when others tell us our problems keep continually not working out for us because of reasons we can't change.

A doubter of God's will for their abundant future will always share their lack of success testimonies. A testimony of failure also comes from a trier when they step out in faith and fail or when they aren't patient enough to finish waiting. A trier thinks, "It can't be my fault if I tried; can it?"

When we feel like we had faith in God and believed something was supposed to happen, and it didn't, there must be a good reason. We tell ourselves that reason must be because someone else prevented it. Faith shouldn't become doubt when we believe in something but want to give up after one try. Just because something didn't happen yet doesn't mean it won't. Perseverance is the foundation of faith for a believer, and the faith of a believer will allow them to try something over and over again because they have faith that God in His time will provide positive results.

Blaming others for our lack of success is a worldly mentality. The world thinks we are supposed to tell everyone that it's not our fault when we don't get what we want. Yes, sometimes believers don't receive what they have faith in God for, but believers won't usually share a story of failure. They may simply say, "God wants that door to stay closed for now." Then, they will try again, or they will try a different avenue knowing that God's will for their lives won't be undone, as it is only postponed until the perfect answer can arrive.

Failure brings doubt. Sometimes our failure is from the enemy to put out our fire of faith. Sometimes, the lack of success is from

God to test our perseverance or to shift us in another direction. In any case, our seeming lack of success is never a final result of faith and should never be declared to anyone as truth.

We can't let stories of failure cross our lips and expect to see victory in our lives. We don't need the temporary comfort or sympathy sharing those stories with the world provides us. We need to seek God's will, put our faith in Him, and rely on His eternal comfort when failure presents itself.

World's Problems

We give testimonies about all the negative things going on around us in the world. We live in a world that shares the defeats of others in order to feel better about our own lives. World problems are easy to point to as the source of trouble in our own lives. Politics, racial strife, economics, and social class issues are just some of the types of issues we blame in our testimony for the lack of success in our own lives or the lives of people just like us.

Our lack of faith in God's will for our own situation to improve is what truly causes our need to share the problems of the world with others.

The enemy knows sharing stories of problems will increase doubt in those that hear it. That's why the enemy made the news. Our country has many 24-hour news channels devoted entirely to the telling of problems, failures, and mistakes of others. We don't see very many stories of God and all the great things He is doing on the news. Instead, we see what the enemy is doing when we hear stories about death, destruction, and lies.

The Bible says the thief comes to kill, steal, and destroy (John 10:10). The news is proof the enemy is doing his job. Thankfully, God's Word also says that Jesus came so we could have a more abundant life and overcome all that work the enemy is doing (John 10:10). Revelation 12:11 says that our testimony is what leads to the overcoming of those problems. However, we use our words to blame each other for why problems are happening instead of believing and sharing our testimony that we are willing to walk in the plan that God has us.

Rather than distributing stories of victory and triumphs, we fill our newscasts, our Facebook feeds, and our conversations with things like death, constant political battles, slander against others, and problems with our economy. As a result, we are basically saying that everything is no good. How can any positive reaction be given to those stories? What sort of faith in God do those testimonies provide?

These stories can only pull down our faith in God. To the world, what we see is what we believe, and the stories we see about death and destruction can only elicit reactions of doubt, fear, and broken promises. To a believer, what we have faith in God for is what we get. God promises an abundant life which is the exact opposite of what the news, and any other negative story will tell us we can have. We need to find faith, and believe that there is no problem in the world big enough to see God provide success in our life, and then we need to share *that* story with anyone who will listen.

Success

Stories of success, especially overcoming hardships to achieve success, are the most powerful testimonies ever told. In order to persevere, we must first put our faith and trust in God. We need to listen to God's will and follow His instructions with our faith. Revelation 12:11 says that we overcome by the blood of the lamb and the word of our testimony. The word of our testimony is mentioned after the blood of the lamb, so that means we get to have our powerful testimony of success *after* we believe Christ died for our sins.

Belief in what Christ did for us on the cross provides our victory over the enemy. Since Christ spilled His blood to cover the cost of our sins, the testimony of His life can be our testimony as well. Since Christ overcame sin, death, and hardship, we can do the same things (Phil. 4:13). The testimonies we share with others about God bringing success in our lives are proof of the victory that Christ died to provide us.

Every time we tell one of those stories it throws more faith in our heart, like logs on a fire. Success stories stoke our fire for God and make it easy for others to see and feel the warmth of the light Jesus shines through those that believe in Him. Every word out of a Christ follower's mouth sends the world a message, and we don't want that message to be words of doubt, but rather we want the world to *know* we can overcome because Christ overcame.

We are supposed to tell others about all that God is doing and will do because a believer *knows* we are promised an abundant life. God has a plan for us, and every time we don't share our negative comments, thoughts, or failures, we are acting with the behavior of a believer. We are expressing our faith without saying a word. Our testimony is being provided by our belief that even though our life may look troubled sometimes, we believe it never is because of God's plan for us to have an abundant life!

Hearing someone tell us how they survived something that should've broken them provides strength for our lives because it allows us to *know* life can get better. Hearing a story of someone working hard and receiving a blessing for his or her effort drives us to put out effort for ourselves. Faith comes by hearing the Word of God, and all these encouraging stories of God's supplied victory in our lives need to be heard.

What stories are you listening to? The promises of your friends and family that tell you the world is tough or that bad things happen for no reason or that it is everyone else's fault? Maybe you listen to the stories of the world that tell you you'll never make it in this economy or that you'll only be happy if you are rich. These things are not true. You should not listen to these voices.

Will you listen to the voice of God? He's the one who made you, and the one who delights in your success (Ps. 37:23). God will provide you with an abundant life if you ask for it (Ps. 16:11). He gives you a hope and a future (Jer. 29:11). God does not want to harm or limit your life but propel it (Deut. 31:8). You hear God's voice in the stories of success because every blessing comes from God (Josh. 23:15). God has a testimony of success ready for your life; you just need to find faith to walk down the path towards God's will and tell the story of what you find along that path to others.

Faith Removes Worry

"People can never predict when hard times might come. Like fish in a net or birds in a trap, people are caught by sudden tragedy." **Ecclesiastes 9:12 (NLT)**

When we go to work, a friend's house, or to the store, we don't usually know *exactly* how long it will take to get there. We just know that it may take ten minutes to get to our parents' house or about twenty minutes to get to work. We don't know if traffic, stoplights, or accidents will increase our travel time. We also don't know if something might happen to keep us from our destination completely.

In fact, all sorts of things can get in the way of us reaching our destination on time. We might crash our car, sit in traffic, or sit at every light for three minutes on the way there. These things can all add time to the length of our trip, but we don't plan for them, we don't desire them, and yet delays will show up from time to time.

Ecclesiastes 9:12 says there is no way to know when trouble will come. Trouble will eventually catch up with all of us, and when it does we will have the choice to either face our problems or succumb to them. Our troubles can be as small as losing our keys or sitting in traffic, as they are big, like a loved one dying or an unexpected loss of a job. Faith in Christ is our only shield against trouble in our lives.

Trouble comes suddenly, and no matter how prepared we are for a trip, or for life, sometimes we break down on our way. When trouble finally comes, we have to take our life on a detour in order to deal with our problems. Taking a detour through our problems may make us arrive late for where we thought our lives would be, and sometimes, those detours may take our life in a completely new direction.

We are constantly facing unexpected trouble. Dealing with that trouble is wise. Worrying about that trouble is not. We cannot act faithfully when we are unsure about how our situation will end. That is the attitude of a doubter and a believer knows that God can handle whatever troubles we are facing (Prov. 11:8).

We are to cast all our worry at the feet of the Lord (1 Pet. 5:7). Our faith shouldn't hinder our lives, but we often let it. We worry about things like how we will pay bills next month, if our relationships will last, and if we will be able to get the things we want in life. These types of worries are common but still need to be given to God.

Our faith in God allows us to live life without worry. We exhibit this type of faith all the time, and I call it stoplight faith. Stoplight faith is the same faith we exhibit each morning we go to work. We leave the house at the same time every day without worrying if we will break down, sit in traffic, or be involved in an accident. We believe every time we leave to go to work we will arrive on time because we've done it so many times before. We have stoplight faith because we know the route, we know the best time to go, and we have had countless trouble free trips.

Stoplight faith knows that there is no trouble that may suddenly appear that we can't overcome. Each morning we leave the house, we believe we won't be late. We also know that if something happens we can deal with it. We know there is a possibility we will run into traffic, or there may be a line at our morning coffee shop. We don't live our lives in worry because we know these things might happen. We should live our entire lives this way because *all* our problems have a solution, and no problem is too big for God to handle.

Our faith in God will remove worry because we *know* our problems are coming, but we *believe* they will be solved by Him.

God is constantly moving and working on our life. The detours God puts us on when trouble comes are there for a reason. Sometimes, it may seem like God has put our life in traffic when we aren't getting to places in life as fast as we would like to be. We shouldn't start doubting or be angry at God because we're not going to get where we are going on *our* schedule. Shouldn't we desire to get where God wants us to go at the time He wants us to get there? God, occasionally, may sit us at a traffic light in our lives, and when He does, we need to be spending that extra time focusing on Him. The extra time we have to spend paying attention to God may allow us to slow down long enough to learn what He is trying to teach us.

When God puts a detour ahead in our life, we need to remember that not every obstacle is disastrous. God knows where He wants us to go; however, the route He takes us on is often not the direction we expect. God likes to do things in our lives to bring Himself glory. We will be exhibiting faith when trouble comes, and we are excited when God receives all the glory for solving our problems. We can only be excited about trouble when we are worry free, and the only way to be free of worry is to find faith in God's will for our future.

Faith Heals Us

"Such a prayer offered in faith will heal the sick, and the Lord will make you well. And if you have committed any sins, you will be forgiven." **James 5:15 (NLT)**

James 5:15 ends the debate about whether or not God is able to heal the sick. He is. The Bible is clear that Jesus paid our debt of sickness at the cross (Isa. 53:4-5). Some people may live their entire lives afflicted, but they will be healed in their heavenly bodies. Some people may find themselves hurting while on this earth, but God may use doctors, medicine, or wisdom to heal them. Some people may find themselves faced with a grave illness or disability and find themselves healed in an instant because God can cure miraculously. **This verse is a declaration of God's love for His people. God cannot tell us any more clearly that faith in the Lord will heal the sick!**

Sicknesses, handicaps, and ailments came into our lives with the introduction of sin. Sickness is the enemy's way of shortening our time on Earth and testing our faith in Christ. God provided an answer to this problem. God provides healing through many avenues including prayer, hospitals, doctors, medicine, and miracles.

When Jesus began His ministry to build the church He performed many miracles. Jesus spoke with great power and served everyone. The Bible highlights the healing faith Jesus used specifically when it gives many accounts of the times Jesus cured the sick and even revived the dead.

There are dozens of written accounts of Jesus healing the sick individually, but the Bible tells us in many verses that He healed *all* that came to Him (Matt. 4:23, 8:16, 12:15; Luke 6:17). Jesus healed leprosy, the blind, the cripples, all the rampant diseases and afflictions of the time, and any other disease or brokenness that was held inside a body.

Jesus was the first hospital.

Have you ever been out on Black Friday? (Black Friday is the term used to describe the day after Thanksgiving that is the busiest shopping day in America.) Can you picture how long the lines of people are on that day to get good deals on televisions, clothes, and toys? There are some people who will camp out for days or weeks so that they won't miss out on a once in a lifetime deal.

Can you picture how long those lines are?

What if I told you there was a line where anyone who stood in it would be completely healed?

Can you imagine how much longer that line would be?

The Bible says Jesus healed *all* that came to Him. How many people do you think He healed? Can you imagine how long it actually took Him *every day* to heal those people? The line you are imagining is the type of line Jesus looked at all the time.

Christ is the only hospital the world has ever had that provides complete relief from all afflictions.

Imagine what it must have looked like when a world full of broken and sick people came from all over to get Christ's healing touch. Just imagine the number of people Jesus actually healed in His life. Jesus would stand there, probably hungry and tired, until the lines were all empty, and everyone was satisfied. Jesus would then do it all over again at the next place He went.

> *"Jesus Christ is the same yesterday, today and forever."*
> **Hebrews 13:8 (NLT)**

Jesus was, still is and will forever be the healer of all.

We know our faith in God heals us, and we also know that not everyone who prays and believes for healing from God receives it in the way they think they should. Sometimes when we use our healing faith we may find that instead of being completely restored God may act in another way. God may bless us with peace over our illness, improved symptoms, or joy to know we are special and that our circumstances will allow us to be used by Him for the greater good. God uses the testimonies from believers who overcome great physical and mental afflictions as a powerful voice for the Kingdom of Heaven.

Healing faith is especially difficult to train and grow in because it can sometimes require great patience. When we pray for healing, and our sicknesses aren't healed quickly, we can become frustrated by our circumstances. We often ask ourselves why our loving God would let us, our family, friends, or anyone at all suffer if He loved us so much.

The answer is simple to understand, but not easy to hear. God isn't letting us suffer. God didn't want for us to be ravaged by sickness and death. Sickness and death are the result of sin. Sin brought sickness and struggle into the world, and it can't be removed until Jesus comes in the last days to finish His work (Rev. 21:4). God brought faith into the world so that we could call on Him to battle against all the struggles sin brought with it. The struggles of sickness are sometimes the hardest times to use our faith in God because is very difficult for any of us to feel peaceful or stay focused on God's future for our lives when our situation is so undesirable.

There is one major reason sickness is such a powerful tool of the enemy to attack our faith in God. Sickness is such a struggle because pain comes with doubt.

Pain comes in many forms and attacks from all angles. Every part of the body is susceptible to pain including every part of the body of Christ. Pain is a constant part of our lives, and it isn't always a physical response to an injury or a symptom from an illness. We feel physical pain in the pits of our stomachs when we are lied to or told bad news, and we also feel pain in our hearts when we are lonely or depressed.

When we are in pain, we begin to doubt. Doubt is the opposite of faith. Doubt is a great weapon the enemy uses to defeat us. When our minds cannot see positive results we begin to doubt. We think things like, "It's all over," "It's never going to get better," or "I'm destined to suffer." Doubts will *always* come into our mind, but they should stay in our minds and never cross our lips because when we allow those thoughts to be heard, it is impossible to be in faith.

The Bible tells us that the words we speak are directly linked to how our heart feels (Luke 6:45). If our hearts believe our struggles cannot be changed, and we speak those words it is a declaration of our beliefs. When we believe things won't work out, we speak doubt, and it is impossible to be in doubt and have faith in God at the same time (James 1:6).

When we are struggling with a negative situation the best thing we can do at that moment is start declaring the opposite of our bad situation. We should say things like, "I am healed and not sick," "I am going to beat cancer and not lose to it," or "This is not the worst news ever and God has a plan for me to overcome this!" Declaring our faith in God for all to hear is something that we can start applying the practice of to our lives today. When we behave this way, we will see God change our circumstances.

In addition to declaring positive words over our negative circumstances, we need to pray for our health before those negative moments arrive. Healing faith isn't generally used until something is already broken. We don't often pray offensively because we have been taught to pray defensively. In other words, we don't often pray and believe for God to keep us from trouble; instead, we pray for help after trouble has made its way into our lives. We *thank* God offensively, but we do not often pray for help offensively, and we need to start.

It is necessary for us to begin utilizing God's help before trouble knocks on our door. One way we start to build our healing faith is by praying about our health while we are healthy: "God, I thank you for healing me. I thank you for preparing a cure, giving wisdom to doctors to find out what is wrong so they can fix it. Thank you for giving me peace and hope that you will resolve my sickness!" This is a proactive, faithful prayer. When we are in faith about our healing, we may find we will go longer between colds or notice it has been a while since we needed Tylenol or visited the doctor. When we notice those small things and begin to thank God for them, it will build our faith.

We know Christ has the ability to heal *all* that ails us. Jesus showed us He heals all our sicknesses when He healed *all* the people who came to Him. Jesus didn't just heal one problem or one sickness. He healed every single one. From the tiniest cold to the death of Lazarus, God healed *all* that came to Him and provided healing faith as payment. The hospital of Jesus let everyone come in, no money, no insurance, and no more problems.

Testimony

I used to get migraines all the time. For around twenty years, I had a terrible headache almost every single day. When I told people, they would say it was stress, a bad diet, or that I simply exaggerated the pain for attention. Every single time I had a migraine and the pain went away, I was euphoric and felt great relief once it was finally was gone. I loved that moment my pain went away.

Until the pain was gone, I always had a hard time believing it would ever leave. I never thought that it would get better. It's not like I thought I would always have a headache, but I didn't have faith in God to believe they would ever stop coming or to make them go right away. That pain I felt from my headaches *always* made me doubt I would get better. That doubt I had because of my pain often kept me from God and my healing even though I didn't realize it.

It took God twenty-eight years to cure my constant headaches, and it took a stroke to cure me. A few days after my twenty-seventh birthday, I went to the emergency room after suffering a T.I.A. or a mini stroke. Testing showed the stroke was caused by a PFO or a small hole in my heart. I had to have corrective heart surgery to repair the hole. Afterwards, the headaches went away. I had lived with them for so long and was so glad to be rid of them. The doctors later told me the migraines I had had my whole life had been a symptom of the PFO.

My stroke happened before I found Christ, but I have no doubt God was the one who healed me. God helped me recover from a stroke, heart surgery, and removed my headaches. God loved me so much even though I wasn't reciprocating that love back to Him. There were also a lot of believers standing in the gap for me with their healing faith, which I appreciate more now than I did then.

I am thankful the migraines are gone. I often pray offensively that they stay away, as well as any other attacks the devil might throw at me. My faith in God's healing is active, and constantly hoping for continued health. After I left my full-time job with benefits to start the ministry, I went more than two years without the need for a doctor or medicine. I eventually did have to see a doctor again because trouble comes to us all, but I believe God kept me away from sickness for that season of life. I also believe the prayers and faith in God from of a believer in my life are what cured me from my life long headache affliction.

We can't let pain dictate our future. We are under attack from the enemy when we are in pain, emotional or physical, and in order to fight off that attack we need to begin to speak the truth of God's Word over our life. God heals *all,* and all we need to do is tell God we need healing! We need to ask God to take sickness from us or give us peace to live with it. In this world, some people will lose their lives early on, some people are born with a hard life right from start, and some people will find great struggles from sickness later on. Hard times aren't reasons to blame God and turn from Him, but rather, hard times provide opportunities to reach out to Jesus for comfort, peace, and healing.

Peace can be given to all, especially those with serious mental and physical problems. God will give us a peace that does not blame Him for what has happened to us, but rather uses our negative situation as an opportunity to glorify Christ. When we are sick or broken, it gives Christ the opportunity to bless us throughout our troubles.

When pain arrives, declare it is healed and believe it is gone. God will prepare our path to healing or peace. We may need to rely on our stoplight faith to be patient while it comes because many things might need to happen in order for us to get better. We might need to make doctors' appointments, have surgeries, or just wait to allow the time to pass to heal. Don't struggle with doubt in those times because doubt could delay our healing.

We know we are using our healing faith when we focus on the moment we *know* is coming. We need to focus on that great relief or euphoria we know comes after pain subsides. We activate our healing faith when we focus all our words and thoughts on what life is like when our sickness is gone. Focus on that feeling of joy God provides to His believers who are focusing on their better future – which is the result of finding faith.

Part Four: What We Need to Know Regarding Faith

Faith Needs to Be Trained

"And now, just as you accepted Christ Jesus as your Lord, you must continue to follow him. Let your roots grow down into him, and let your lives be built on him. Then your faith will grow strong in the truth you were taught, and you will overflow with thankfulness."
Colossians 2:6-7 (NLT)

When you start a new job, you must be trained. Being a new Christian is a lot like starting a new job. We don't know many people, have lots of questions, and are unsure about many things relating to our new Boss. Paul addresses the newness of becoming a believer in Colossians 2:6-7.

Paul tells believers there is more to being a Christian than just accepting Christ as Lord. We are told here that our foundation is to be built on, and around, Christ so that our faith in God will be strong. Our foundation includes anything that is important to our life including our families, jobs, interests, and our worship. We are supposed to include God in all of these major points of lives so that we can be built on Him. Once we are strong in faith Paul writes that we will overflow with thankfulness. Thankfulness is evidence of joy, and joy comes from finding faith to follow God's will.

We need our faith in God to be trained in many ways, so that we are able to use it properly to do all the different things He will ask of us. Training our faith isn't much different than training for our jobs. We train for our jobs because our employer wants to know that we are capable of following directions. An employer wants us to understand what to do and how to do it, and those aren't always things we know before we walk in the door. We wouldn't be able to walk off the street, without experience, and do the job of a trained professional better than they do; however, we constantly think we can do a better job at managing our lives than God does.

When we face trials, we are very quick to assume God can't help faster, or better, than our own efforts. We don't always want to live our life constantly asking God to fix what we broke, and it isn't always easy going to Him in every situation. So, instead of asking God for help, we try and handle our situation, good or bad, by ourselves. It is *always* easier to let God handle things, instead of doing them ourselves. God wants us to train our hearts, our minds, and our words to be faithful and patient.

If we aren't allowing God into all our situations, it means our foundation isn't in Christ. We can't have strong faith in God without the foundation of deep roots that come from sharing *every* part of our lives with Him.

God has the only perfect solution for our problem. Limiting God from doing His job limits the blessings of our life. When we use our faith, only God knows what to do to see our life perfectly rewarded. Putting faith in our own abilities to make decisions can disable instructions from God on the choices we should be making instead. That time we waste carving our own path can delay His movement and blessings in our lives. God wants to be in charge of our lives no matter how small the problem. Constantly inviting God to be involved in our lives can sometimes be hard to do, but when we do involve God we are training our faith, and making it strong, so that we can be overflowing with thankfulness and joy.

The keys we use to train our faith in God will be in our possession when we gain knowledge about some of the basic questions we have about faith. We cannot attain understanding of any subject without first gaining knowledge, and there is a lot to learn about faith. Once we understand how faith in God works and how we are supposed to use it, we will see our faith grow strong. Learning and implementing new ideas and procedures into our routine can take time, but they are essential in building our foundation of faith around God.

Training our faith is no different than being trained for a new job. We may find it difficult at first to complete certain tasks. However, after we train at a new job, we will eventually be able to do things on our own without instructions or help. Once we find ourselves working on our own for an extended period of time, we will find ourselves doing tasks very quickly and efficiently that we previously needed guidance to complete.

The results of trained faith aren't usually evident until we become comfortable in our surroundings. When we become new believers, we have to embark on a brand new relationship with Christ, share our faith with the people around us, and make life decisions based on our new beliefs. It isn't until we become comfortable in our new life and get into our training that we will begin to know what we need to do in order to be efficient at finding faith to do God's work.

Once we train by gaining knowledge, our keys will allow us to know what faith is and how to use it. After our training, we will become more efficient at our workplace, and we won't need to be reminded to use faith because we will just know God can unlock doors for us by using our keys of faith.

Keys to Training Our Faith

- **Why do we need faith?**
- **Why do we need to give God thanks, faith, and glory?**
- **What tools did God give us to work with?**

Why do we need faith?

Training our faith begins with gaining the knowledge that we need faith because of where we are. Our workplace to do God's work by faith is here on Earth. However, the boss at our workplace is currently not God. Satan is in charge of Earth, and as long as Satan is in charge, things on Earth are always going to go bad, and we are always going to be under attack.

In the beginning, God gave possession of the Earth to Adam. When Adam sinned, he handed over possession of the Earth to the devil. God cannot take back from the devil what He gave away to Adam without first sending Jesus to take the punishment for that original and all subsequent sin. That is why Christ had to die for our sins. Since Christ died while being sinless Himself, authority over Earth reverted back to God. Christ will one day return to remove Satan from power, and Christ will rule and reign over Earth (Rev. 20).

Christ will return to defeat Satan, but until He comes, Satan, *not God*, is the temporary god of this planet (2 Cor. 4:4). That is why everything on this Earth is dying. Satan is the reason why there are wars, natural disasters, and terrible things always happening in the world. God is not the one doing these things because Jesus has not yet taken control over Earth. If Jesus was in control of Earth, He is currently doing a terrible job running the workplace. The enemy is in control of Earth and is trying to destroy every one of us.

It is because Satan has authority of this Earth that we need faith in God to see His will done in our lives. Faith in God is our only weapon to battle the enemy with while we are on the Earth.

While Jesus is *not* the current Lord over this planet, He is the Lord over our bodies, our minds, and our spirit. We make Christ our Lord, which means owner, when we believe He is our savior. As our Lord, Christ will provide our lives with abundant peace, joy, and blessings if we use our faith to rely on Him. Our faith allows God into our lives to fight those battles on our behalf. All we need to do is thank God and give Him all the glory for all we are and have.

Our God is the God of love and redemption. God has a plan to send Jesus to remove us from this situation on Earth, but until that day comes, we have to train our faith by knowing why we need it, and where we need to use it. Faith in God is our weapon to solve problems. God gave us faith to storm the gates of Hell. When we wake up in the morning and still have problems, it means Jesus hasn't come back yet, we are still under attack from the enemy, and we need to use our faith in our Lord to fight back.

Why do we need to give God thanks, faith, and glory?

God has given us many things including life, plans, gifts, and our savior Jesus Christ. Our job on this Earth is to worship God, and we do that by being thankful. We need to thank God by waking up every morning and putting our hands in the air to praise Him. We need to thank God for letting us be in this world, but allowing us to no longer be a part of it because we are now a part of the Kingdom of Heaven. We need to thank God for making us a priority in His life by making God a priority in our lives. We need to make Christ our Lord by asking Him to guide our steps that day, and we also need to *believe* in Him for something *every day*.

God wants us to use our faith every day, but we will usually stop using our faith to rely on God if we feel like everything is working out for us. That's one reason why God sometimes doesn't answer prayers until they *need* to be answered. God wants us to use our faith all the time, and if He dumped all our blessings onto us in one day, we would stop relying on Him. God isn't a lottery ticket.

God wants us to give Him faith that we will be married, but God may not provide us with our spouse before we are ready for them. God wants us to use our faith to be blessed with money, so we can be the lenders and not the borrowers, but may not show up with millions of dollars to support us forever. God loves us and wants to be our provider, but our desires may not always meet His provision. God wants us to keep Him as a daily part of our life because He knows only faith in Him can protect us against the attacks of the enemy.

God desires the glory. God deserves the honor for all He does. We have done nothing and cannot boast about our own efforts, but must boast about what God does for us (Ps. 44:8). We cannot train our faith properly without complete understanding that faith is founded in the belief that only Christ deserves honor for any reward, accomplishment, or success our faith in God provides (Phil. 4:13). **We train our faith in God by constantly being thankful for Him, believing in Him for something *every day,* and noticing when that faith is rewarded by giving God the glory.**

What tools did God give us to work with?

Every day we will wake up under attack, some days are easy to fight back, and some are going to be really hard. There is good news though. God has equipped us with armor and tools to fight off attacks. Faith is a powerful part of our work tools, but it's not our only one.

The struggles of our life on this Earth did not come as a surprise to God. He created all the tools, and weapons, we will use to fight and protect ourselves with in our battle against the enemy. The tools God gave us to work with on Earth are clearly stated in Ephesians 6. In this chapter, Paul lists all of the armor that God gifted us with to battle the enemy.

God gives us access to this armor at all times, but we don't always put them on. The freedom of choice that God gave us means that when attacks come, and we face them without God, we will be facing those battles all alone and without our armor. We can do anything we want, whenever we want, but there will always be consequences, good and bad, that will come from our decisions. God won't force us to use our armor and it is up to us to choose whether or not we will use the tools God has given us to be successful in our battles against the enemy.

> *"Finally, be strong in the Lord and in his mighty power. Put on the full armor of God, so that you can take your stand against the devil's schemes. For our struggle is not against flesh and blood, but against the rulers, against the authorities, against the powers of this dark world and against the spiritual forces of evil in the heavenly realms. Therefore put on the full armor of God, so that when the day of evil comes, you may be able to stand your ground, and after you have done everything, to stand. Stand firm then, with the belt of truth buckled around your waist, with the breastplate of righteousness in place, and with your feet fitted with the readiness that comes from the gospel of peace. In addition to all this, take up the shield of faith,*

with which you can extinguish all the flaming arrows of the evil one. Take the helmet of salvation and the sword of the Spirit, which is the word of God. And pray in the Spirit on all occasions with all kinds of prayers and requests. With this in mind, be alert and always keep on praying for all the Lord's people. Pray also for me, that whenever I speak, words may be given me so that I will fearlessly make known the mystery of the gospel, for which I am an ambassador in chains. Pray that I may declare it fearlessly, as I should." **Ephesians 6:10–20 (NIV)**

All of these pieces of armor have been fitted to our personalities, our gifts, and our talents. We can all use every single one of them. God gives them to us, and they fit perfectly for our use. For the purpose of this book, we will only be highlighting verse 16, and spend time learning about the Shield of Faith that God gives us.

"In addition to all this, take up the shield of faith, with which you can extinguish all the flaming arrows of the evil one." **Ephesians 6:16**

What is a shield? It's not a weapon, but rather a piece of protection. A shield provides cover from the attacks of an enemy. If we were to think back to biblical battles we might picture the men fighting with large swords and heavy shields. Those types of battles were prominent in the days Paul wrote this letter highlighting our tools from God. Paul knew the importance a shield had to a soldier in battle. Shields in those days were often heavy and difficult to carry, but men took them into battle because they needed to have a way to defend their lives.

Our lives are constantly fighting attack, and we need to use our shield of faith to protect ourselves. Soldiers knew their shields were important, and they were likely trained to use their shields before they went out for war, so we also need to train in the use of our shield of faith by gaining knowledge about its importance. That knowledge will train us to carry our shield of faith with us every day instead of leaving it at home because it is too heavy and difficult to carry.

First, we need to learn why our shield is important. We learn why in the end of verse 16, where it says our shields are meant to extinguish the *flaming arrows of the evil one*. Flaming arrows sounds scary, and the Bible tells us that the enemy wants to shoot arrows *at us*. In fact, they don't just want to shoot arrows, but they want to light them on fire first, and then shoot them. The enemy not only wants the arrows that hit us to burn us, but also to burn the ground around us we're standing on.

God uses this illustration to tell us how big the problems we are going to face look like. God is letting us know the enemy isn't going to stop. When we think of arrows, we don't just think about one arrow, but instead, we think about a quiver full of arrows. The Bible doesn't use the word sword here to describe the type of attack we will be facing. God isn't describing our battle against the enemy as one terrible blow, but rather multiple constant attacks that are meant to destroy us completely.

Fiery arrow attacks don't just affect our lives, but will also come against everyone standing around us and the land we occupy. That means our friends, family, and other people in our lives are all vulnerable to being affected by the attacks coming at us. For example, an entire family can be affected by an attack that caused the job loss of one person. Friendships can be destroyed because of the addiction of one person. The attacks we face on our own, will often affect the people closest to us. Thankfully, God tells us not to worry because all of us can be protected against these attacks by using the tools He gave us.

We are protected when we exhibit faith in God's will for our lives. Faith is our shield. Verse 16 gives us hope to say that our shield not only protects us, but also *extinguishes* the fiery darts of the evil one. According to dictionary.com, the word extinguishes means to put out something that is burning or giving off light or to end something. What a wonderful word Paul uses here to describe what our shield of faith provides us.

During the Sermon on the Mount, Jesus describes believers as the light of the world meant to shine bright for all to see (Matt. 5:14). The enemy is trying to extinguish the light believers exude. God tells us the opposite will be true when we use our shield of faith. Carrying our faith will extinguish, or put an end to, the attacks from the enemy. It doesn't matter how many problems, or fiery arrows are headed our way today, our shield of faith will *always* stop them.

Faith, like a shield, may be uncomfortable and heavy to carry at first, but we will get strengthened through our practice using it. We also may not like the way faith looks on us at first, but it is just like a uniform and the tools we have to wear at any new job; eventually, we will become used to it. If we leave home without our badge for work, we just have to turn back and get it. If we forget our shield, we'll have to train ourselves to remember to go back and retrieve it. When our shield of faith becomes a daily part of our life, joy will become a daily part of our life as well because *knowing* we are protected from fiery arrows will put hope for God's future for us in our heart.

Faith Needs to Allow God to Answer Prayers

"They cried out to God during the battle, and he answered their prayer because they trusted in him. So the Hagrites and all their allies were defeated." **1 Chronicles 5:20**

I once heard a Christian joke that goes like this:

A levee broke near a river, and the waters were flooding the town, forcing everyone to evacuate. The police came up to the most religious man in town and said to him, "Sir, you'll have to leave your house!" The man said, "No, I'm not leaving. God has always helped me before, and He will do it again." So as the water started to rise, he went to the second story of his house when another boat came by, and the driver of the boat yelled out, "Sir, you'll have to get on this boat or you're going to drown!" The man replied again, "No, God helped me before, and He will do it again."

The water rose even higher. This time he went to the top of the roof, where a helicopter came and flew overhead. The pilot called down to the man, "Please climb on the ladder or else you are going to drown!" The man continued to say again and again, "God is going to help me!"

The water rose higher and higher and soon he drowned to death. The man went to Heaven, and there he stood and asked God, "Why didn't you help me?"

And God said, "I did help you; I sent you two boats and a helicopter!"

This joke has a basis in truth. Our faith for God's will in our lives can be grown or diminished based on our own perception of its results. When we pray and ask for God's help, we are asking God to move in our lives because we *know* He has the power to provide an answer to our cries for help. Our faith increases or decreases based on how we think God should respond versus how God actually responds.

For instance, one of the most common prayers we pray is for God to bless us with financial help. We pray for help to overcome the struggle of debts, have more money, or have better paying jobs, but we often don't recognize God's blessing in those areas because the blessing doesn't happen how we expect.

When we pray for financial blessings, we hope for a million dollar blessing or to find great success easily. Our perception is that those are the ways our faith in God should allow a financial blessing to arrive. Blessings won't often show up that way. Instead, God may offer a path to bless us with more money by allowing us opportunities to pick up extra shifts at work or by giving us an entrepreneurial idea. It doesn't mean financial help didn't happen; it just means we may have missed them while we were waiting on our exact expectations to arrive.

When we put our faith in God's will to be done in our lives we need to allow God to answer our prayers the way He desires without using our expectations as the guidelines for success.

1 Chronicles 5:20 tells us the Lord answers the prayers of the people who trust Him. Dictionary.com defines faith as confidence or trust in a person or thing. Our faith in God's will is defined by our ability to put our trust into His plan. The men in this verse who cried out for help from the battlefield were facing a battle where they should've been defeated. The only way they could find victory was through God. They found victory because they trusted God, *and* also because they didn't have an expectation they wanted God to use. Those men didn't care how God granted them victory over the Hagrites, they just knew God would do it. Our faith needs to *know* that God answers our prayers, but also *know* He will answer them in His way.

We can apply this knowledge to our faith by asking God for things *every day and trusting He will do it*. God doesn't want us to use faith sometimes or most of the time; He wants us to use it *all the time*. God doesn't want for us to waste our faith, however, we limit God's will to be done in our lives when we only try and put our faith in Him on the really hard days. We miss out on wonderful things when we treat faith with unimportance.

Think back to earlier in the book when we discussed that birthday present we bought someone. Remember, we are excited to see someone open a gift we gave them, and even more excited if he/she was so enthusiastic and thanked us for it. We would also be hurt if he/she acted unexcited and discarded our gift. What if he/she never used it more than once or twice? How happy would we be if the gift we got him/her became his/her *favorite* toy or possession? What if he/she used it every day and told everyone how cool it was or what an awesome gift giver you were? Wouldn't that make us want to give that person more gifts because we see how he/she appreciates it?

All the feelings of joy those moments bring us are the same feelings God has when we use and appreciate our faith in Him to work in our lives. When we are using the gifts God gives us, He gets excited. It makes God happy when we start showing off His gifts to others by telling them how cool our God is and all the things He does for us (Rom. 11:11).

When God sees us being thankful, He in turn, wants to get us more gifts, and bless us with more exciting things to play with because He knows we will appreciate it. Not only will we be happy by receiving more blessings, but the people who see the cool things we receive from God will seek Him out to find blessings in their own lives. They will then get their own gifts by seeking God out for themselves, and using their faith in God's will to receive what He has for them. The good news is that there are more than enough blessings to go around. God has an endless storehouse that He uses to bless everyone who comes and asks Him (Deut. 28:12).

Our world as a whole mostly has a lottery mentality. We want it all, and we want it now. We don't want to have to worry ever again, and we want to feel secure. That "our way" mentality the world has is what sin nature looks like. Our faithful prayers don't get answered the way we want, they get answered the way God decides. Our nature is to want God to give it to us our way, but that isn't how God makes us feel secure. Our security should come from God's love, and not from money, or any other possession we perceive as valuable.

If God answered our prayers the way we wanted Him to then we wouldn't need Him anymore. Faith would be unnecessary and so would God. God teaches us to rely on Him because He deeply desires to take care of us every day. We learned when we examined the different relationships in our families about the hurt that can occur when we don't feel needed or wanted anymore. We, too, can hurt God by not letting Him love us the way He wants to—which is to give all the time.

We *know* our faith is working when we change our behavior to rely on God's will and not our expectations after we pray for God's help. Behavior, not our words, is how we show our true faith in God. The man from the joke was very religious, and many people heard about his reliance on God, but no one saw it. He drowned waiting for God simply because he expected things to happen his way and chose not to see it God's way.

When we accept God will answer our prayers His way, we will never stop seeing His help for us. It is up to us to either take what He has to give, how He wants to give it, or to rely on ourselves to provide our perceived good result.

Our faith is payment to get God working in our lives, but prayer is the way to activate that faith. Going to God early, often, and openly is the evidence of mature faith. We need to carry our keys of faith with us to be able to produce that mature faith. Our keys to getting prayers answered establish a foundation of knowledge, which understands how God responds to our faithful prayer.

Our expectations need to be on the same page as God, so that we can recognize when our faith in Him is being rewarded. We get on the same page by equipping ourselves with the fundamentals of how God answers us when we go to Him in prayer. Without that knowledge, it will be very difficult for us not to set our own expectations and possibly miss out on what God has for us. Finding faith in God's will comes from acquiring a belief that God will provide, but we need to know how, so that our faith perceives the right results.

Keys to Getting Prayers Answered

- **God Doesn't Answer to Our Sin Nature**
- **God Always Shows Up Right on Time**
- **The Answer Will Always Bring Glory to God**
- **God Sends Us on the Road Less Travelled**
- **God Supplies Us with Wisdom and Grace**

God Doesn't Answer to Our Sin Nature

Our sin nature causes us to desire immediate answers to our prayers, and it has a hard time trying to be patient while waiting for God to act. Sinful desires cover all selfish behavior and are not limited to things we might categorize as *major* sin like premarital sex, drunkenness, or lying. The sin nature that causes those types of sins is the same nature that makes us not want to go to work, drive faster than the speed limit, and eat food after we are full. When we pray, we are often trying to feed this sin nature.

We see sin nature reveal itself a lot in our lives. We see sin nature manifest every time we see a child throw a temper tantrum when they aren't getting what they want. Some of us might say that is just a kid being a kid, but we act like that as adults, too. We have hopefully matured enough to stop crying when we don't get our way, but just because we aren't crying doesn't mean our tantrums stop. We will complain, curse, get angry, yell, throw pity parties for ourselves, mope around, or get offended when we don't get things our way. We are just as likely to do these things when they mess up our order at the drive through as we are to do them when someone who is unqualified gets the promotion we wanted.

When we pray, we are often trying to ask God to give us what we want. We ask for more money, better health, and

for other things to satisfy our desires. However, our heart in prayer should be to see God's will be done in our life, and not our will.

The difference between our will and God's will is how our answered prayer will serve others. When we pray, it is okay to ask God for things for ourselves because the Bible is clear about God wanting us to lay our worries at His feet, but also for us to share the desires of our heart with Him (Ps. 37:4). It is the heart in which we ask for things in prayer that needs to change. When we request something from God, we should not be trying to satisfy our sinful nature, we should be trying to satisfy God's plan for our lives, which is to love God and serve others (Mark 12:30–31).

For instance, it is our sinful nature to pray for financial blessings simply so that we can feel secure by a large number in our bank account. God does not answer prayers from our sin nature. If we are praying for God's will to be done in our lives, our prayer might be to ask for more money to provide food for our children, to get out of debt, or to be able to give more to the church. Both prayers are asking for more money, but they are asking with a different heart.

We will always be fighting with our sinful nature in prayer. We are selfish people because we were born into sin. The Bible tells us that once we become believers we are no longer of this world, and should pray to God as believers that desire God's will above our own (John 17:6–19). God's Word also tells us that our joy in the Lord can be fulfilled by faithfully becoming Christ's disciples (John 17:13). In other words, our joy comes from being faithful to following God's will for our lives. God will answer prayers, but it is up to us to pray with a heart to see our desires met because our desire should be to please God and want for our lives what He wants to provide us.

God Always Shows Up Right on Time

God loves making an entrance. God loves to show off and answer our prayers right on time, not a second too soon or a second too late. Our sinful nature has a hard time with this because our pride wants to take credit instead of God, and also because our sin nature is not very patient. Our lack of patience is a symptom of sin that causes us to doubt. Doubt disables our faith in God and won't allow our prayers to be answered.

Thankfully, God knows it is *very* hard for us to be patient, and that is why patience is one of the fruits of the Spirit (Gal. 5:22). God gives us these fruits, or gifts, to help believers have the ability to stay in faith towards His will longer so that our prayers can be answered at His right time. Patience is essential for our faith to work, and without it, we will all eventually embrace our sin nature. When we are not patient, we will not allow for the promises of God to take hold in our lives, and then we will turn to our own thoughts and actions to accomplish the things we are too selfish to let God handle.

> *"So the Lord must wait for you to come to him so he can show you his love and compassion. For the Lord is a faithful God. Blessed are those who wait for his help."*
> **Isaiah 30:18-19 (NLT)**

What we need to know about faith in God is that it requires us to wait. Isaiah tells us the faithful are blessed when they are patient while waiting for God's help. We will all find ourselves being impatient from time to time, and that impatience will occasionally lead us to making decisions on our behalf that are not in God's will.

It is important to know that if we make a mistake and try to answer our own prayers through our own actions, we must repent quickly and turn back to God's plan. Remember, God will never leave us, and He has the power to turn around anything we did. God turns mistakes into miracles.

God gives us Biblical examples to remind us He forgives our mistakes, like when Abraham had a son with Hagar. God forgive Abraham for His sins, and He blessed Ishmael and his descendants. That was a mistake that turned into a miracle. God's Word also tells us that the answers or blessings to our prayers may not be right around the corner, like when Jacob waited fourteen years for Rachel. Prayer doesn't always get answered when we think it should, but God is good to answer prayers, even when it feels like eternity between the time we prayed, and the time we found God's provision.

We will constantly need to have our shield of faith up for long periods of time in order to keep our blessings from being taken from us by the enemy. God loves us, and His Word tells us He won't give us more than we can handle (1 Cor. 10:13). So, we should be encouraged to know that our prayers will be answered before our shields become too heavy to carry. When God does arrive with our answer, it is always in perfect timing, but sometimes it takes longer than we want. God takes His time, so that He can build our endurance, patience, and humility. Our faithful prayers for God's will to be done in our lives will be answered, if we allow God to do it on His timetable, and not our own.

The Answer Will Always Bring Glory to God

We are meant to worship God. We worship Him by sacrificing our time in prayer, Bible reading, fasting, singing, and other ways. When we worship God, we are giving Him praise and honor. God created us, and our purpose on this Earth is to worship Him. Worshipping God is a common theme throughout the Bible and answers the question why we were created. We were created to worship (Col. 1:16).

God wants us to worship Him, but we have been given the choice to worship whatever we want. The Bible describes people making idols and worshiping them, and that is still happening today. An idol is anything we worship or something we devote more time, attention, and desire to be with more than God.

Our sin nature sometimes takes our attention off of God and puts our focus, or our worship, on other things. We often worship our children, spouses, money, and entertainment although most people wouldn't call it that. We would just call those things important. Anything that takes importance in our lives *above* God is an idol. We may not call the people or things we care deeply about a god or an idol but we do sometimes worship them.

Our faith in God's will needs to know that when we get a prayer answered through a blessing or an opportunity it will always bring glory to God. We cannot provide blessings for ourselves because all blessings come from the Lord through our faith (Deut. 28:2).

Sometimes, God answers our prayers in a way that makes it very easy for us to glorify Him. Sometimes, even faithful prayers won't get answered because they don't serve God's will. Sometimes, we receive what we think are blessings, but are not part of God's plan for our lives.

For example, perhaps a person gets a promotion at work. Promotions are generally considered blessings. What if that job disgraces God's purpose for their life, or goes against His morals or ideals. Is that promotion a blessing? Is that where God wants them to be? Will that promotion cover up that feeling they still have to want something more for their life?

Our real promotion, or our something more in life, will come when we begin to have faith to go where God wants to put us. When we understand that the answers to our prayers are meant to glorify God, we will look for those answers to come. We will worship God by praying for our desires to glorify His kingdom. We can find joy in whatever answer God designed for our prayer because He knows all our needs, but He just needs us to ask. We need to let the answer to our prayer bring attention to our great God.

God Sends Us on the Road Less Travelled

Gods tells believers that the road we take is a road less traveled (Matt. 7:14). Our journey will be harder to walk than the path everyone else will take. However, the reward for taking this path will *never* be outdone by anyone that is on the other path, no matter how it seems.

When we find faith to ask God to guide us in our lives, He will often respond by sending us on this road less traveled. God will answer our prayers by asking us to do things we

may not be comfortable with so that we will need to lean on Him to walk by faith and not by sight.

This will not be easy because our sin nature will fight to serve ourselves above God. However, when our faith is firm in the Lord, and we do walk on that road God made for our lives we will see God increase our faith, stretch our endurance, and test our patience.

God's will for our life and the faith we will need to use to embrace trials come from an understanding that even though our road is tough, it is the better direction to take. Many will look for the wide road that leads away from God's will. Any road we take that doesn't follow Jesus will be met with uncertainty, hard times, regrets, and misfortunes. We need to take the road less traveled because Jesus paved the way down that road while dragging a cross on His back.

When we pray for God to answer our prayers, we need to be on the lookout for that road less traveled. God may answer our prayer for more money by providing a great paying job that requires us to take many more years of schooling. God may answer our prayer to be free from addiction by letting others stop bailing us out, and let us face the consequences of our sin. God may answer our prayer to have children, or a spouse, by making us go through adoption, or by choosing a spouse for us that we didn't have in mind.

When we learn to take the road less traveled after we pray, we will begin to find faith in God to reach the end of that road, and we will find the answer to our prayer waiting there next to Jesus.

God Supplies Us with Wisdom and Grace

When God responds to our prayers He will often provide wisdom and grace as the answers. When we understand how prayers are answered, and how faith is rewarded, we will begin to see they all come from a place of wisdom and grace.

Our faith in God needs to be rooted in the knowledge that wisdom, and grace, are as much an answer to our prayers that answers of support, resources, and healing can be. When God answers our prayers by giving us wisdom, He is giving us the ability to understand a subject better, in

order for us to make better decisions. When God answers in grace, it is a blessing that requires no work to receive.

What does a prayer answered with wisdom look like?

Let's say someone is praying for God to provide them with a house. Instead of just providing a house, God may give the wisdom to first find out which house they want. Next, God will give them the wisdom to know how much money they need to make at their job in order to pay for that house. Then, they will receive the wisdom from God to know that they now have to perform better at work in order to receive the higher salary needed to pay for that home. When they take possession of that home, it is because they used faith in God given wisdom to receive God's will in their lives.

What does a prayer answered with grace look like?

Grace simply means receiving a gift we did nothing to deserve. For example, salvation is one answer to prayer that only comes from God's grace. Peace, patience, and all other fruits of the Spirit are also answers to prayer that come from grace. God answers prayers through grace, when we pray for God's help in times of great need. Grace is supplied when there is nothing we could possibly do to change our situation. Grace is the answer we receive when we pray for God's will to be done in our lives in areas like salvation, grief, and depression.

Our prayers aren't always answered in the same way. Sometimes we need patience; other times we need to look for the moments that bring glory to God to find the answer to our prayers. We will also need wisdom to follow His instructions for our life, and the grace to live patiently while we expect them.

God responds to the prayers of His faithful people. God wants us to ask Him for help, and God gives us those things we ask for in abundance (Prov. 2:6). To receive God's response all we need to do is ask. If our faith isn't spoken, it isn't activated. The same way words of doubt disable faith, encouraging words activate it, and increase its growth. Prayer is the number one way to start using words that activate God. Start thanking God for wisdom, long life, riches, and honor. Thank God for grace to be patient, while He prepares our future of abundance. Thank Him for the joy our faith finds while we are waiting for prayers to be answered.

Testimony

I've personally had lots of prayers answered in ways that I never saw coming. I want to share one with you to illustrate how God answers prayers, and also how He prepares the path for us to receive His will in our lives.

When I was living a completely lonely life without Christ I thought a woman, a girlfriend, or a wife was the ultimate answer to that emotion. I thought companionship would cure all of my emptiness. I didn't even begin to understand the giant hole I had in my soul was meant to be filled with the love of Jesus and the Holy Spirit and not by the love or attention of a woman.

When I first became born again, it was still the number one prayer request I sent up to God. I was not alone in wanting someone special either. It seemed like every single person I knew had one thing on his or her mind, the opposite sex. This was multiplied when I spoke with Christians. Most Christians know God promises us a good thing, or a spouse, so they have faith to receive one. However, when that person doesn't arrive as soon as they ask, Christians have a tendency to doubt God has someone for them, or they think that He isn't listening. They don't understand when they begin to doubt they are canceling out their faith.

Truly, God prepares our future to coincide with His will. Our constant faith that God's promises are on the way are what bring them, and they will probably not arrive while we are angry and doubting God. Having stoplight faith is crucial in these situations because God's answers always have obstacles, including time, for us to hurdle. Our faith in God to overcome the hurdles puts us in a position to receive the answer to our prayers in the way He desires and brings glory to Him.

From the time I got born again, I often prayed for God to send me a wife. On days that I would get angry with God because I spent the night alone or with no one to talk to didn't help my cause. I couldn't avoid the doubt in my head sometimes, but I knew I needed to let that doubt disappear and to not speak it out loud. However, my sin nature prevailed, and I spent a lot of nights vocally doubting God by not understanding why He hadn't given me what He promised.

Then one night at church everything changed for me. That night, I heard a sermon from a guest speaker named Joe McGee. Joe taught about marriage. That night I was already mad about something unrelated and didn't even want to be at church. I almost didn't go, and when I heard Joe say he was going to talk about marriage I got even hotter. I had no girlfriend, no prospects, and the last thing I wanted to hear about was how great marriage was.

God works in unexpected ways though. It was during that sermon, on a night I didn't even want to be at church, I heard a message on a subject I didn't want to hear about, that I learned many things, which changed my thinking and the course of my life.

Hearing God through Joe that night is still the single most influential sermon I've ever heard. As Joe spoke about unfamiliar things, I was drawn to listen. I learned so many new things that night, about faith and marriage, the importance of our praise life, and moving in God's direction for our lives. The things God showed me that night ended up strengthening my faith so much that I am now able to walk on God's path for my life today.

After that service, I began to get involved volunteering at church, instead of just attending. I start tithing, and I also started praying differently. I began thanking God for things I had instead of asking Him for things He had not given me. As Joe talked, God gave me knowledge on how to be a spiritual leader of a family, and how love is about giving your life to supply the needs of someone else, and not just about finding someone who "has to like me for me." I heard Joe say, if we are stubborn enough to think we are already perfect (which I did) and think we don't need any help, then we are not teachable. When we are not teachable it means we aren't humble, and God wants us all to be humble. I wanted to be different for God.

I heard that sermon in February 2013. I began studying marriage and realized I didn't actually know why marriage was important to God. I was thankful to find out. I then began to pray and also thank God for the wonderful God fearing woman He was preparing for my life. Even though I had yet to receive her or even meet her, I knew she was on the way, and I was grateful.

In March of that year, God called me to the ministry, and a few weeks later He gave me a vision of the woman who would be my wife. God showed me in a dream that I would meet her on the street while she was wearing something strange on her head. God also told me she would be a vital part of my ministry and would give something to me when I desperately needed it.

I met the woman God had prepared for me on May 29, 2013. We met on the street outside a coffee shop. Her name was Megan. She had some sort of fancy headband on. She later told me she had been wearing a headband, and a bandana, on her head most of the day because she was part of a photo shoot earlier in the afternoon, and it was the only time in her life she ever wore those two things. Megan eventually became a vital part of my ministry, and more importantly, she gave me something so crucial when I needed it most.

Soon after I started my ministry, many people I knew doubted my calling. I was called a baby Christian and was told many times, "God doesn't call new believers to start ministries." Many people vocally doubted how and what I was hearing from God and told me I wasn't doing the right thing. It shook my faith in God almost to the point of quitting. What

Megan gave me that was so important was an overwhelming encouragement to keep following after God's will.

Megan inspired me to find the faith to know it didn't matter what others said, only what God said. It really strengthened me because I was a recently born again believer with a troubled past who was much older than her. Megan had no earthly reason to stand behind me or have faith in my God-given call, the visions I received, or what I was believing for God to do through the ministry. She easily could have left my side quickly without any remorse. Something others encouraged her to do often until the day we were married. Yet she stayed. Megan was crucial because she encouraged my faith in God by demonstrating faith in God.

Megan showed stoplight faith by knowing where she wanted to go, but not planning for all the things that might stop her from getting there. I am blessed to now be her husband.

Looking back, I can see more clearly all that God did. God was preparing things the entire time, and He was also preparing me. When I met Megan, she was able put her faith in me because she saw how God had changed and blessed me. As we began to get to know each other, I realized how much more God did than I ever realized when I heard the testimony of the prayers she was sending to God before I arrived. Megan had also been thanking God for the man He was bringing to her. She prayed and believed God would send her a man in ministry, and someone who would be a spiritual leader.

If Megan and I would have met a few years before we did, she would've been too young for me. If we had met many months before we did, I wouldn't have an understanding of God's giving love, nor the ability to share that kind of love with her. If we had met a few weeks before we did, I wouldn't have yet been called into ministry, and I would not have been the man she expected. What if God had answered my prayer for her on my timetable?

Our prayers for a godly partner in ministry were answered but not exactly packaged the way we thought. We have to give God all the glory for answering our prayers in His way because we are blessed and absolutely had nothing to do with how we came together and eventually married.

Months before I met Megan, my faith in God's will for my life led me to start tithing, get involved in church, start the ministry, volunteer, and start making budgets. Without all the corrections and changes God had made in my life, I would not have been prepared to receive Megan as my wife.

God was always with me. I just needed to see past my circumstances and find faith in God's will for my future that included a loving spouse. God was always preparing things behind the scenes. God prepared Megan's heart to receive a recently worldly man, and He prepared me to be the Godly man she desired.

Faith Needs to Mature

"Don't copy the behavior and customs of this world, but let God transform you into a new person by changing the way you think. Then you will learn to know God's will for you, which is good and pleasing and perfect." **Romans 12:2 (NLT)**

Paul paints a clear picture for believers to see in this verse. Our behavior is not supposed to mirror the customs of the world – which is to act selfishly because of our sin nature. Instead, we need to change our behavior to serve God and others. However, we can't change our behavior in our lives without first changing the way we think about it. A change in thinking is the first step to maturing our faith. When we begin to change our thinking to be Christ-minded, we will find our faith being matured.

Paul, the author of Romans, uses this verse to explain that we need God to transform us by making us new. When we change our thinking about Christ, we become a new creation and find pieces of ourselves start to chip away to reveal a new person.

Finding faith in God's will establishes a change in our thinking so that we will not desire to exhibit worldly behavior. Our transformation into a new person will never cease as long as we continue to change our thinking. The maturation process of a believer is known as sanctification.

Sanctification, or our process of transformation as a believer, is a lifelong process and begins when we exhibit the ability to change our thinking to align with God's will. We first exhibit this ability when we change our thinking about Christ and receive the gift of salvation. Changing our faith to grow in maturity is no different than changing anything else in our life – which is to change our thinking to match God's will.

We change our thinking to match God's will by acquiring knowledge. To acquire the knowledge of God that leads to maturity, we first need to acquire Christ as our savior through repentance and faith. Once we find Christ, it takes time for Him to teach us through sanctification. Jesus needs to teach us how to hear Him, and we need to learn how to listen. The longer we believe in Christ and do what He is asking us, the more changes He will be able to make in our hearts to mature our faith.

Whether we've been born again five minutes or fifty years, faith in God can *always* be improved and worked on. If we learn new things that change our thinking, we shouldn't be upset we didn't already know those concepts *and* be living by them. It is okay to find out we don't know everything!

God wants us to learn, and we should trust Him to show us what areas we are strong in, ask for grace and wisdom for the areas we need to work on, and humble ourselves to learn things we have no clue about. When we do those things we will allow for maturity to take place in our faith, but it won't always be easy.

We like to use the terms growing "pains" to describe growth in areas that are being strengthened. Sanctification may bring growing pains, too. When we start walking in God's path for our lives and realize we need to change our thinking, it may be painful because we may think we already tried what He was asking us to do, and we don't want to go down that hard road again. We might hurt because we can't understand why God wants to change our thinking in order to take away something we think we should be able to keep in our lives.

Have you ever seen a parent take something away from a child because it is dangerous? That child will cry even though the parent is doing it for the best. God is our parent, and sometimes He needs to take something away from us because He knows it is dangerous. When God takes something away from us, we may act just like a child by being upset, crying about it, and not understanding why He did it.

The Bible tells us when we face these situations, we aren't supposed to lean our own understanding, which is the same as worldly thinking, but rather, we are to put our faith in God's will for our lives (Prov. 3:5).

Testimony

During my ten year gambling addiction, my choices ruined many good parts of my life and reduced those ten years to a memory that's not worth having. There is not one moment I can remember being happy during those years. In fact, most nights I went to bed I hoped I wouldn't wake up. When I found Jesus, I wasn't doing anything right. All I did was change my thinking about Jesus, and the rest of my life transformed.

However, everything I needed help with didn't get fixed overnight. I still had problems I didn't want to face. I didn't stop gambling right after I was born again. It took several months, continued missteps, and many wrong choices before God delivered His grace for my addiction. There are still many areas where I am changing my thinking and my faith to match God's will, so that I will transform my behavior.

In order to mature our faith we will first need to discover what the problem is that is keeping our faith from overcoming. Then we will need to discover the answer from Christ in order to implement change.

Transforming our faith through sanctification may hurt, just like withdrawal from any old way to a new way hurts. When we break up with someone it hurts, when we start working out after a year on the couch it hurts, and when we start doing things for Christ when we are used to doing things only for ourselves, it will hurt. Hurt doesn't mean things are bad; it just means we are growing.

We need to add some new keys to our keychain. Keys are the ideas that help us understand faith, so that we can change our thinking about them. Romans 12:2 says once our thinking is changed, our faith can mature into something God can use to carry out His will. We are also told in that verse to be mindful of our thoughts because they should not agree with the thoughts of the world. The keys we will gain to grow our faith will come from knowing how the world views faith.

To see our faith mature, our thoughts must be far away from worldly thoughts, but we need to know what they are so we can recognize if we exhibit worldly behavior. We are not meant to think like the world; we are meant to have the mind of Christ, and Christ says that nothing is impossible through faith in Him. These keys are how the world tries to limit our faith. Christ says faith is limitless and produces abundant blessings. If we find ourselves thinking these ways, maybe we need to humble ourselves to know we need to change our thinking, so that God can mature our faith to be doers of His will.

Keys to Improving Faith

- **Faith is Only for Salvation**
- **Faith is Only for Big Problems**
- **Faith is a Coincidence**
- **Faith Didn't Work Before**

Faith is Only for Salvation

Faith does refer to a necessary part of the process of salvation; however, having faith, *also* refers to living a life reliant on Christ. Faith isn't limited to one use only, but the world believes faith's sole purpose is to get people into Heaven.

When a believer has faith, it is more than the belief that Jesus Christ is their Lord and savior. A believer knows because of God's Word that faith is used to see God's will happen. Faith guides our prayers, our thoughts, and our behavior, so that the will of God is done in our lives.

God wants us to know that we carry a key of mature faith when we understand how big faith produces big results. Jesus said, with faith anything is possible, that faith moves mountains, and little faith can throw deep rooted problems into the sea (Phil. 4:13; Matt. 17:20; Luke 17:6).

The world may see people with who have faith as simply being people who believe in Jesus, but we shouldn't degrade something like faith to mean just one thing. Faith can provide many things in our lives. The same faith we use to receive salvation is the same faith we use to receive peace, a spouse, a job, or any other blessing inside God's will. Faith in God's will produces results in a number of ways and having that knowledge will mature our faith to believe God can do *all* things in our lives.

Faith is Only for Big Problems

While most people are drawn to Christ most often in times of despair, stress, and pain, those things should not be the only reason we should seek him out. The world will tell us that God doesn't want, or is too busy, to be a part of our daily lives, but that is not true. To mature in our faith, we must begin to rely on God for all our problems.

God wants us to know that we carry a key of mature faith when we understand that Christ deeply cares about every part of our lives. God knows how many hairs we have on our head, and that number changes every day (Luke 12:7). If God is counting the hairs on our head every day, it seems like God is watching over every detail of our life, not just our big problems.

We need to mature our faith by improving our daily relationship with God. We need to go to God often and for all reasons including being thankful, and not just go to Him for help when things get bad. When we begin to rely on Him for everything we will strengthen our faith, and when the hard times do come, we will be much more mature in our faith and ready to deal with them.

Faith is a Coincidence

When God answers prayers the world will often believe it is a coincidence, or a result of mere chance. Having faith in God's will to be done, and then receiving a blessing for that faith, is never a coincidence. When the world calls faith rewarded a coincidence, it takes the glory away from God, and instead gives the glory to luck. Luck did not supply every blessing in our lives, God did.

If we asked someone to bring us lunch, and they brought us lunch, would we call it a coincidence? Why then, do we ask God for blessings and call it a coincidence when He provides them? Is it God or luck that should get the glory for our blessings? Is it easier to believe that God, the creator of the universe, or luck, a random set of events that no one could have predicted, provided our lives with blessings and joy?

God wants us to know that the key to mature faith is knowing that God is responsible for our abundant blessings, and the Bible tells us God will bless us by providing our every need (2 Cor. 9:8).

The world wants to believe that our needs are supplied by our own hands and abilities or something as random as luck, but God's Word says otherwise. To mature in our faith we need to change our thinking to *know* that we deserve no credit for the victories in our lives. God is precise in His actions to bless us, and they are not random. Responding to God's blessings by being thankful in prayer or sharing our testimony are ways we behave with mature faith and show that we have changed our thinking to be like Christ.

Faith Didn't Work Before

The world believes that when bad things happen to people of faith, it is proof that God doesn't answer prayers. The world will notice when a Christian dies tragically. The world struggles with faith when they watch people pray for healing, and it doesn't arrive. The world notices when a believer doesn't get a promotion. Each one of these situations provides the world with ammunition in the battle against God, but the world thinks we should have everything we want. God doesn't always answer prayers in the way we want.

The enemy uses our perceived lack of results as a weapon of doubt to destroy our faith in God. Our doubts are reassured when we think our faith already didn't work or at least that's how we see it. The Biblical definition of faith is to believe that we *know* what will happen even though we haven't seen the outcome of it yet (Heb. 11:1). So when we believe something can't happen because it didn't happen before, we are agreeing with our doubts. When we think this way, our doubt is multiplied.

God wants us to know that the key to mature faith is the knowledge that the past does not define the future. God's Word tells us that finding wisdom provides a better future, and that we will not have our future hopes cut short (Prov. 24:14).

We mature our faith by gaining wisdom, and we gain wisdom through gaining knowledge. Knowledge is what allows us to change our thinking, and in turn, changes our behavior to follow God's will. Mature faith comes from expecting good no matter what, but the world will often remind us how bad our circumstances are, or were, so that we stay hopeless. Mature faith is assured that the problems we are facing today have no bearing on our future, and that our future, regardless of our past or present circumstances, is full of hope.

Part Five: Using Our Faith

Get Our Faith Flowing

"Whoever believes in me, as Scripture has said, rivers of living water will flow from within them." By this he meant the Spirit, whom those who believed in him were later to receive. Up to that time the Spirit had not been given, since Jesus had not yet been glorified." **John 7:38–39 (NIV)**

In John 7:38, the Bible says that anyone that knows Christ as Lord will be filled with living water, and verse 39 says Jesus meant living water to mean the Holy Spirit. Why would Jesus describe the Holy Spirit as flowing water? When a body of water stops flowing or has nowhere to go, it will end or die, like the Dead Sea. Jesus described the Holy Spirit as rivers of living water because He is flowing in us, and, therefore, will never die. Our faith in God's will needs to flow in our lives just like our Holy Spirit does.

The Holy Spirit lives inside those that know Christ as Lord (1 Cor. 3:16). The Holy Spirit is our wise counselor, and we will be able to understand His counsel because He lives inside us (John 14:16-17). To keep faith flowing, the Holy Spirit will be necessary to walk in God's will because of the conviction the Spirit brings (1 Thess. 1:5). Through conviction the Holy Spirit makes believers aware of their sin and leads them to repentance. In other words, the Holy Spirit helps us change our thinking, and we change our behavior to faithfully follow the will of God.

To use our faith in God properly we must understand that we grow our small faith into big faith, much like waters begin in a small creek and become part of the ocean. We

grow our faith and keep it flowing with continual use of faith for God's will to be done in all areas of our lives.

Having faith every day for God in the small areas of our lives, which may include meals, transportation, or projects at work, will eventually supply the big faith needed to overcome loss, separation, or doubt. Our faith is flowing when we are using it, but we need to constantly be using it, so that it doesn't die.

That is why it is so important to use our faith for the small areas of our lives. If we only wait to use our faith in God when big trouble comes we may wait too long, and our faith won't be able to flow into that area of our lives because it is dead. Our faith should never be at rest.

Our keys to faith in God are now going to shift from ideas in God's Word that promote change in our thinking to keys that unlock faith in our lives through our behavior. As we move forward and gain methods of practical application of faithful behavior in our lives, these keys will be the landmarks we use to remember how to get our faith in God flowing in the area where He needs it to be.

Keys to Letting Our Faith Flow

- **Faith Needs to Be a Habit**
- **Faith Needs to Be Spiritual**
- **Faith Needs to Be Observed**

Faith Needs to Be a Habit

Faith, like going for a run, is easier to do when we do it more than once a year. A runner becomes able to run faster and with endurance through continued practice. We need to use our faith in the same way. Using our faith regularly may not be easy, but the results will always be seen, even if it is only incremental. Like a runner who starts training for a marathon by running one mile and months later is able to run twenty. The wonderful whole result of their training when seen from a distance is only able to happen because it was transformed by increments.

The key to making our faith become a habit is to include God in our lives early and often. We should begin by waking up every day and spending time in prayer, and asking God to show us what we need that day or how we can use our faith to walk in His will. The everyday habit of trying to come up with new ideas to pray for will stretch our faith and allow God's will to flow into new areas of our lives.

Our faith in God will begin to get stronger, like a muscle, when we exercise His will in our lives. The more things we are asking for, the more results we will see from our exercise. The faster we see results, the faster we grow our faith. As time goes by, God will answer us and we will be able to start checking off things on our prayer list, and those victories are a result of flowing faith.

Challenge:

> Wake up every day and believe God will answer your prayers. Find a partner and share your daily requests with one another. Try a spouse, roommate, sibling, friend, etc. Get two people in agreement on your beliefs, and God will move on them (Matt. 18:19). Write them down on a calendar, text, e-mail, notebook, etc. Writing it down will give your requests life, and make them more than just a thought in your head that you may forget.

Testimony

> When I had quit my job to follow the path God laid out for me, there were many times I woke up with no food in the fridge and no money in the bank. I would have to wake up every morning and thank God for providing my food because I had no way to do it myself. When God provided and I crossed food off of my list every day, it built my faith.
>
> It was a real stretch for me to have to believe in God for food. I had never prayed for food before. I never really had to. My money took care of those needs when I was working. My

faith was in my money to buy food. God really wanted me to rely on Him for everything, and this is just how He started to teach me that. It was very tough at first, not to ask others for help, but I would simply pray every morning and believe somehow I would eat. I also tried to remember that if I didn't get to eat that day there must be a reason for that, too.

As the days went by, and I would wake up and pray for food, God continually answered my prayers, but He kept showing up in creative ways. Some of those blessings included receiving calls from friends who offered to buy me a meal, I was given groceries, invited to BBQ's, and my roommate would often share his leftovers. I wasn't going around calling people and asking them for things, but rather I asked God to be my provider, and I trusted that He would bring food for me from somewhere. I always believed that if God wouldn't provide for me that day, I just wouldn't eat; however, I never missed a meal. When God always provided I would cross food off of my list every day, and it significantly built my faith in God to be my provider and that faith in God started to flow into others areas of my life.

Faith Needs to Be Spiritual

Trusting the Lord is a spiritual event. Our sin nature is designed to trust ourselves first, and others second, if at all. Putting our faith in God first, and not ourselves or others, is impossible without faith. Faith in the Holy Spirit is what will empower us to do the will of God.

The key to making our faith spiritual is to understand that God's will for our lives cannot be taught or learned, only shown to us through the Holy Spirit. To have spiritual faith we need to ask God to reveal the secrets of God, Jesus, and the Holy Spirit to us, so that we can be anointed to walk in God's will for our lives.

We will need to ask for spiritual faith because it can't be gained just by reading the Bible. There are people who have read the Bible, but they are not saved because they lack the spiritual faith to overcome man's need to understand something before they believe in it. We need to understand that spiritual faith must exist to be in God's will, but understanding how an event occurs following the use of that faith, including spiritual blessings, doesn't make them happen.

I don't understand how televisions, phones, or airplanes work, yet I see them work. I don't understand how miracles happens either, but I have the spiritual faith flowing in my life, which opens me to recognizing when they happen.

Spiritual faith can only come when our beliefs match the truth, and it is God who reveals the truth to us (Matt. 16:17). God will reveal truths to His people without asking, but we can also gain truth by asking God for a spiritual revelation to occur in our lives. When we are aware of the conviction of the Holy Spirit, it will guide our faith to move, or flow, into the right area of the will of God so that we can be used by God in the way He designed us.

Challenge:

> Learn, understand, and *know* that you are anointed by the power of the Holy Spirit to follow God's will, and to be a doer of His Word (Acts 10:38). Pray and ask God to open your eyes to the Kingdom of Heaven, and for His anointing to abound in you. Then go out and use your anointing and faith for God's will to be done in your life so that you can do mighty things for the Kingdom.

Faith Needs to Be Observed

Every time we put our faith into something, we have to wait on the results. Sometimes, our help is immediate, but most times, having faith also requires having *a lot* of patience. The more time that passes while we wait for big blessings to come will give more time for the enemy to attack our faith.

The key to making our faith be observed is to understand that all blessings need to be recognized and treated similarly. We need to recognize God giving us successes in small areas of our lives just as much as we recognize His significant blessings in our lives. Recognizing all the blessings in our lives, and knowing they came from our God that cares for us deeply, will give us the endurance to carry our shield of faith longer and allow our lives to be filled with constant joy.

Our daily lives are full of observable situations to increase our belief in a positive future for our lives. Small blessings are an important part of the perseverance of our faith. When we take small blessings for granted, the enemy uses that time to encourage us to believe we are not being blessed. However, God is continually blessing us, but it is up to us to recognize God's work in our lives.

We are quick to forget the small blessings of God because we always want more and aren't satisfied with the things we have. If we think we have a present left to open, a vacation still to go on, or an exciting meal coming up, we tend to put all our excitement in those things to come. Looking forward to the future God has for us is faithful, but when we only look for giant blessings it leaves us lacking joy. Our joy is connected to where we believe our future is headed, but joy manifests in our present lives. The Bible says we are supposed to have joy in our present standings, as much as we have hopeful joy in our future (Rom. 5:3; James 1:2; 1 Pet. 4:13).

Pretend you have a big birthday event planned, and it will be a giant celebration with all your friends and family in attendance. Your birthday event will be a day full of all sorts of food, fellowship, and fun.

Now, pretend several things happened prior to that big celebration day:

- Your spouse got you a really thoughtful gift.
- Your family treated you to a special dinner of your choice.
- Someone took you to see a movie to celebrate.

When the day of the big event arrives, you are so excited. You arrive at the party dressed well, and they spend the next couple hours celebrating you. You open the gifts everyone brought, they tell loving stories about you, they sing you a song, and they present you with your favorite cake. Everyone has a great time, and it means a whole lot to you that they all came, gave you gifts, and told you how awesome you are. You sincerely thank them all for coming, and you will honestly treasure the memories of that day for a long time.

When God answers our big prayers because of our faith we observe the results like this party, and we put a lot of emphasis on our big blessings.

Big blessings, or prayers answered miraculously, from God are the sorts of events that happen only once in a while. They are met with great fanfare. We usually tell everyone we know about it, "Hey, look what God did for me!" We want to sincerely tell everyone how much their time and prayers were appreciated while we went through the struggle before the blessing. We will treasure the memories of that big blessing and tell that story of faith rewarded for the rest of our lives.

During our celebration and thankfulness for the big blessings in our lives, we sometimes overlook the other blessings that took place as well. For instance, before the party we were treated by family and friends to a special dinner and a movie.

If those moments were real, all of them would probably get overshadowed, and underappreciated because of the big birthday event. The gifts they gave you were good, and you might remember them, but not in the same way you'll remember that big over the top experience of that party in your honor.

After a big miracle in our lives arrives, we need to be as thankful for the prayers people spoke over us, the conversations we stayed up to have with others in our time of worry, or the little financial gifts that helped support us before our promotion as we are for the miracle itself.

Our faith in God needs to be observed. When God blesses our faith with time for a family dinner or money for a night at the movies, we need to be experiencing thankfulness on a level that isn't so far removed from how we act when God provides a miracle in our lives. Our faith will begin to flow when we start to notice, appreciate, and share the stories of how we had faith in God to provide the small things in life. Our faith in God's will to be done then increases in our lives because we aren't dependent on a once in a while giant event to get us through tough times. We need those little moments to help keep us going until the big moment.

Our faith in God's will is a like rollercoaster and for every giant drop of big blessings, there are a bunch of little blessings that aren't as exciting but are still part of the ride. Our faith will grow when we use it regularly by recognizing all blessings. Declaring our small things as important brings focus and honor on to God and, in return, will bring blessings and rewards in our life. When we are faithful with the little things, we will be faithful with the big things (Matt. 25:23).

Challenge:

You can get your faith flowing by using it to be thankful for small blessings. I recommend doing this challenge to force yourself to recognize small blessings, and also to put them on the same level in your life as the big blessings. Get a stack of thank you cards. Fill out those cards over the course of a month and give them out to many people in your life, all the while being thankful for the little things.

You can call your parents to talk about your life, and then write them a thank you card, just for being good listeners. You might write in a card to thank a coworker because they helped you out by switching shifts. Leave a note thanking the mailman for blessing you with mail every day. When we begin to share our thankfulness to people for the unnoticed, small blessings that they do every day, we will be able to recognize all the little, unrecognized things God does in our lives. Finding time to be thankful to God for all He has done for us will allow us to find faith for all God will do for us!

Advertise Our Faith

"So never be ashamed to tell others about our Lord. And don't be ashamed of me, either, even though I'm in prison for him. With the strength God gives you, be ready to suffer with me for the sake of the Good News."
2 Timothy 1:8 (NLT)

Have you ever been out to eat with someone, and when he/she takes a bite of food, grimaces and says, "This tastes terrible; here, try some?" Does that food sound appealing?

When a person wants us to try some of his/her food based solely on the terrible description, we would probably refuse. However, if he or she simply says, "I didn't like this very much, but you might," our decision may be different. It's all in the advertisement, and our words are used to describe our food as well as our savior.

Timothy writes in verse 8 that we should never be ashamed to advertise our faith in the Lord. Our savior Jesus Christ should hold the highest importance in the life of a believer. We will spend our lives telling others about our family, friends, and children, and we need to share our stories about our love for Jesus as well. We cannot be afraid to share with others that we love Christ. We need to make it a priority to introduce our relationship with Jesus to others.

It won't be easy to share the nature of our relationship with the Lord. Timothy tells us we will need God's strength because we will suffer persecution for the sake of our relationship with Christ, but it is also our job as believers to share the good news Christ came to bring. Thankfully, Timothy doesn't stop by telling us all we will do is suffer, but a few verses later, Timothy writes that if we endure those persecutions as believers, it will be because Christ knows us and we know Him, Christ will not deny us, and we will reign with Him (2 Tim. 2:12).

Advertising our faith for God's will to be done in our lives starts with gaining the knowledge that one of the ways we advertise our faith by is by how we speak about our lives. Once we know that our words correlate with our faith in God, we must then understand that the words we choose make a big impact on what happens next in our lives. To use our faith correctly, we should be advertising our faith positively *all* the time.

However, outside of Christ, staying in faith all the time is a task that will never be accomplished by anyone. We are sinful people, and everyone, including the apostles, can become victims to lack of faith. Peter, as described in the gospels, used His words to deny Christ on three separate occasions.

When we are under attack, even if our thoughts are doubtful, it is what we say out loud that will become the description of our situation, and those words will lead to what happens next. When our life is good, it's easy to say nice things about God and have faith for the unseen future He has for our lives. However, sometimes a situation is so miserable, heartbreaking, and hard to understand why it is happening, that it may become very difficult to stay positive. Even in those situations we need to learn to try, and use positive words to advertise how we are relying on our faith in God to get us through our circumstances.

The Bible tells us that our negative emotions are not supposed to be our guide in life, and that we should not be living our lives based on how we feel when things go bad or wrong (Col. 3:8). The Bible also tells us that we are supposed to live by faith, and not by sight (2 Cor. 5:7). When a problem presents itself, small or large, our words are the problem solver.

Our words are meaningful because there is life and death in the power of the tongue (Prov. 18:21). Our words have the power to direct God's future for our lives before we take one step in any direction.

Gaining knowledge and understanding about how to advertise our faith in Christ are just the first steps to using our faith correctly. Next, we need to collect the keys we can use to behave differently; once we change our thinking to believe God has a plan for us, we need to advertise to the world that we have faith in our relationship with God. The keys to advertising our faith will allow us to be able to share God by giving us the tools we can use to stay positive during hard times, grow during times of calm in our lives, and allow our faith in God to be used on a daily basis.

Keys to Advertising Our Faith

- **Stay Positive Starting Now**
- **Learn to Be Quiet**
- **Speak God's Word**
- **Be Content**

Stay Positive Starting Now

Our words bring into existence what we want to happen. If we want to go out to dinner with someone, we will first ask them if they want to go, if they do, we will then go get dinner. If we want God to answer our prayers, we must first use our words to ask Him, and then, if it is in God's will for our lives, He will answer our prayer. However, to see God move in our lives, we will need to stay positive in our faith through our words.

The key to staying positive in our faith for God's will to be done is to not say things when we speak, even jokingly, that are the opposite of what we actually want. Instead of sharing negative thoughts, we should submit our requests to God, and wait for Him to answer so that we can focus our time on staying positive and thankful.

For instance, if we want a new car, we shouldn't say we can't afford it, it's too expensive, or only if we win the lottery. Our words take hold when we say them, and if we say we can't afford something, we probably won't be getting it.

We also won't get that promotion at work by saying, "I'll never be the boss" or "I'm just not smart enough to do that job." Those negative words impact our thoughts and put us in a place that is in the opposite direction of the receiving line for that promotion (2 Tim. 2:16).

We need to use our faith to let God know how excited we are to receive all the answers He has for our prayers. We do that by letting everyone around us know we are believers by saying things like, "That car is going to be mine," "God is going to show me how to budget for it," or "God will give me grace for the patience to wait for it!"

We can start being positive about life right now, even if we have been negative for a long time about something. There are things in our lives that linger, and we have a hard time speaking positively about them. We often see positivity being a problem in many situations, including child custody battles, divorce proceedings, and for people battling physical disabilities or mental handicaps.

Many of us deal with long term illnesses, disabilities, or diseases, and it can be very difficult to stay positive during very tough trials such as those. Having medical issues also leads us to continually advertise our health, and we use words like, "I'm always sick" or "I live at the hospital." These words have been spoken over our lives by our doctors, families, and us. Words like that aren't in faith, but often go unnoticed and are seen as venting words.

God's Word tells us that we say what we believe (Luke 6:45). We wouldn't say we were sick all the time if we had faith in God's healing. If we tell people we want to be healed and then tell them how sick we are, we have disabled our faith. Instead, we can advertise our faith by telling others God has put us on a path to recovery. We can let everyone know we are expecting great strides in medicine to cure whatever ails us. Our positive words of faith will directly impact the results of God's will on our lives.

We need to move on from our negative attitudes about lingering situations and start using positive thinking right now. We need to ask

God for forgiveness, and also for wisdom and grace to stay positive in situations that are hard for us. Once our thinking changes, our behavior will follow. If we believe our situations can be handled by God, we will share those beliefs with the world because the Bible says out of the heart the mouth speaks (Prov. 4:23). The Bible is telling us we use our mouths to advertise our faith in God.

When we use positive words to advertise our faith in God, we are expressing our hope that we will be rewarded with positive outcomes. We need to take out the negative declarations we use over today's circumstances and focus our speech on the future that will come from God tomorrow instead. Use words that include what will happen and not what *is* happening.

Challenge:

> Try to remove common negative expressions from your life. We commonly use negative phrases to describe our finances like, "I'm broke," "I don't have the money for that," and "I don't know how they expect me to pay that when I only make minimum wage." These negative words disable our faith and don't allow the blessing to start its course to your life. Instead of saying those things, focus on the future and what God's will can make happen by saying things like, "God thank you for the new job that will raise me out of poverty," "Thank you God for the wisdom to spend money more wisely," "Thanks God for the discount I received on my bill," or "I know God can help me pay off these debts and start saving."

> Your faith in God starts and ends with what comes out of your mouth. When you are positive and believe the future God has for your life holds no limits to your current situation, you should be advertising that news with others. Advertising your faith in God will lead to other's wanting to find faith in God for their lives.

Learn to Be Quiet

Being quiet may seem contradictory to the idea of using our mouths to promote faith, but it can be a very powerful tool in our armory. Learning to stay quiet may sometimes be the only way to stay positive because sometimes, it's just too hard not to say the wrong things. When trouble comes all the positive words in the world won't stop our minds from thinking the worst. We might think, "This is never going to happen," "I am a failure," or "How am I going to figure this out?" These are all the wrong thoughts; however, they are still in our minds.

The key to advertising our faith in God is sometimes best done through quietness. Negative thoughts don't disable doubt, negative words do, and if we are unable to use positive words of faith, our best tool to overcome an onslaught of negative thoughts is to stay quiet during the storm. Our quietness won't allow negative thoughts to turn into negative words.

The Bible says out of the mouths of two witnesses a thing is established (Matt. 18:16). So, if we say we are broke, even jokingly, and someone agrees with us; then, we're broke. To keep that from happening we need to stay positive. If we can't say, "I'm rich", even if we don't believe it, it is better to say nothing at all.

Negative thoughts are a fiery dart attack and will always come because the enemy is trying to get us to say them out loud. The enemy knows the power of our words, even if we don't. The second we speak the negative thoughts the enemy planted in our head, we have immediately disabled our faith for God's will to be done in our lives. Our faith can't contradict itself; we can't say something won't happen and still believe in our hearts that it will.

Staying quiet does not produce the hope that speaking God's promises and scripture will; however, staying quiet will not allow negative thoughts to turn into negative words and attitude. Being quiet will prevent negative actions from taking place because our mouths won't come in agreement with our doubt. We need to prevent negative actions because they could lead to the possible delay or even the removal of God's answer to our problems.

Challenge:

> Use quiet time, to try and hear from the Lord. Advertising your faith is vital to the success of sharing the gospel with others. How you describe your circumstances lets others perceive your faith and decide if they want the God you love. If you are facing a difficult situation, you'll need to be spending quality time with the Lord to work through it, so as not to let others perceive weak faith that doesn't believe Christ can do *all* things.

> When trouble comes, leave the thoughts of doubt in your mind, and just stay quiet. Use that quiet time to hear from God by listening for His instructions on how to face your problem. The more you are able to reflect while you are quiet, the easier it will become to produce the positive words needed to believe in a brighter outcome. You will constantly be battling the enemy with your words, but sometimes saying nothing is a more powerful way to find faith for God's will to manifest in your life.

Speak God's Word

Another key to advertising our faith is to declare God's Word out of our mouths. No positive word that comes out of our mouth will ever be as important as any scripture that calls for God to move over our lives. God's scriptures are unfailing promises to us (Gal. 3:21). When we faithfully speak scripture over our lives we bind the attacks of the enemy, and those fiery darts will be extinguished (Matt. 4:10-11).

We know God's Word binds the enemy because Jesus battled the devil by speaking scripture over His circumstances in the wilderness. This section of scripture is the instruction manual Jesus gave us to build our faith that speaking God's Word will defeat the attacks of the enemy.

> *"Then Jesus was led by the Spirit into the wilderness to be tempted there by the devil. For forty days and forty nights he fasted and became very hungry. During that time the devil came and said to him, "If you are the Son of God, tell these stones to become loaves of bread." But Jesus told him, "No! The Scriptures say, 'People do not live by bread alone, but by every word that comes from the mouth of God.'"*
>
> *Then the devil took him to the holy city, Jerusalem, to the highest point of the Temple, and said, "If you are the Son of God, jump off! For the Scriptures say,*
>
> *'He will order his angels to protect you. And they will hold you up with their hands so you won't even hurt your foot on a stone.'" Jesus responded, "The Scriptures also say, 'You must not test the Lord your God.'"*
>
> *Next the devil took him to the peak of a very high mountain and showed him all the kingdoms of the world and their glory. "I will give it all to you," he said, "if you will kneel down and worship me."*
>
> *"Get out of here, Satan," Jesus told him. "For the Scriptures say, 'You must worship the Lord your God and serve only him.'" Then the devil went away, and angels came and took care of Jesus."* **Matthew 4:1–11 (NLT)**

Jesus taught us that God's Word is successful in defeating the attacks of the enemy. Jesus didn't respond by saying "God, you need to help me"; instead, Jesus declared God's Word because He knew that God is moved to action when scripture is declared through faith. Jesus taught us that no amount of begging, pleading, or crying will get Him to change our situation. God is not moved by pity. God is moved by His Word (Isa. 55:11).

If we don't know why our life is a hot mess, then we probably don't know what the Word of God says about getting us out of our troubles. When we gain knowledge of the fact that God promises us a long abundant life full of riches and honor (Prov. 22:4), we will then be able to ask Him to provide those things for us (John 15:7), and then we can faithfully expect for their arrival (Titus 2:13).

Challenge:

1) Speak God's Word over your circumstances. God gave us promises through His scriptures, and He wants to fulfill those promises to us, but we have to speak them in order to see them manifest in our lives. Jesus gave us the example, He spoke the Word of God, and His faith in God's Word manifested victory over the attacks.

2) Discover God's promises over your situation. God has promises to make us overcome all our troubles. God has promises for money trouble (Prov. 8:18), relationship reconciliation (2 Cor. 5:18), and forgiveness for our sins (1 John 1:9). Learn one of those verses or find your own and declare God's promise over your life in that area. Prepare yourself with the knowledge of God's Word so that you are able to use it as a weapon to fight off those fiery arrows. God moves on his Word. When you find faith to speak God's Word, you *will* receive God's promises.

Be Content

Delayed blessings are still blessings. Imagine the twenty-five years Abraham and Sarah spent between God's message of many children and the arrival of their son Isaac. We think we wait forever sometimes to get an answer or a blessing from God. Twenty-five years is a long time. Abraham was under a constant struggle from the enemy to doubt what God had promised Him. Abraham was in doubt so much that he tried to help God fulfill His promise by acting in a way that produced Ishmael.

If the father of our faith had a hard time staying content, we should trust God knows we are going to have a hard time also. Thankfully, God can encourage our faith to be patient so that His will may be done in our lives. Our lives won't easily stay satisfied, but we should strive towards the will of God and be content no matter what troubles we may be facing in our lives.

The key to advertising our faith is to understand that God's will is for us to be joyful wherever we are at in life. Our words and behavior should not act as if our lives our troubled because God's Word says our troubles will not touch us, if we have reverence for God, and live in content (Prov. 19:23).

The will of God is not for us to be depressed because we are in a bad marriage, we have a terrible job, or for any other reason (Phil. 4:11). If we are depressed, it is because we aren't living with faith in God's promises that things will get better. If we are depressed, it means we are in doubt about something.

Seasons come and go. It's easy for us to be excited for our birthday parties, but harder to advertise excitement for our siblings' birthday parties. It's always easier to get discouraged than it is to be encouraged. Faith and our circumstances don't always match up, and the enemy uses those moments in life to discourage us and move us away from God by attacking our faith to believe in His promises. When we are in doubt, the enemy is in control, and things will not work out for our good. When we are in faith, God is in control, our shield protects us and nothing is impossible.

Challenge:

Be satisfied. You have daily opportunities to be content wherever you are. God promises your troubles cannot touch you when you are content, so you will need to find ways to be satisfied. Find a mundane, boring, or tedious part of your life and find ways to be faithful in advertising satisfaction in those activities.

Try advertising to others how much you enjoy the job God has given you instead of complaining about working. You could try to sing songs to God while running errands or cleaning the house. Praising the Lord with a full heart is a sign of contentment (James 5:13). We need to remember that God has planned out our victories, and all we need to do is stay content, not use our own efforts to fulfill God's promises on our own, and stay in faith long enough to allow God to fulfill them instead.

Deliver Our Faith

"Do not be anxious about anything, but in every situation, by prayer and petition, with thanksgiving, present your requests to God." **Philippians 4:6 (NIV)**

I remember going to the post office when I was a child, our family station wagon would sit there waiting in a line three cars back to drop mail in the slot of a dark blue bin that held outgoing mail. It was a real treat when my mom would let me be the one who put it in. I always felt good afterwards, like I had been chosen to do a special mission.

Not only were the bins lined up in front of the post office, but they could also be found scattered all around town. The blue bins were always next to the now almost extinct newspaper bins in front of the grocery stores and on random street corners. Those blue bins were a staple of the post office, and when we dropped of our mail in one of those, we *knew* it would get where it was supposed to go. It didn't matter if the bin was in front of the post office itself or the one down the street.

We learned to put our trust, hope, and faith in the postal service. Yes, sometimes mistakes may happen, but time and time again, the post office delivers our mail on time to the place we want it to go. We trust that the prices are the same no matter which one we go to. We believe when we hand the post office an important piece of mail, it will get where it needs to go.

Philippians 4:6 says we are to present our requests to God, and we are to do it without fear or anxiousness. We already exhibit this faithful behavior towards the post office, but we need to change our thinking to put more trust in God.

To deliver our faith to God, we must give over control of our circumstances to Him without fear because we believe our situation will get where it needs to go. To use our faith in God correctly, we need to believe that we will be delivered from our problems, but that requires us to let go of our desire to be in control of our outcomes. God cares for us, and His ways are better than ours, so we need to find faith to trust in His will for our lives (Ps. 118:8).

We exhibit faith with our mail, and we just need to transfer that thinking over to our faith in God. Our faith in God should *know* that He will deliver us from our problems. When we hand off our mail to the post office, it is because we don't have the time to deliver it ourselves, and we don't care if they deliver our mail by bus, car, or train as long as it gets there. Imagine if we actually had to drive to all the places we send our mail to get them there. Doing that would take up all our time and wouldn't really be a realistic way to do things, but many of us approach our faith in this same way all the time. We try and do things the hard way.

Instead of giving our faith to our postman (God) and dropping it of in the blue bin (prayer), we drive it where we think it should go. We make our own choices about how and where it ends up. That usually puts delays in our lives, but if we were to put the same faith in God that we do for the post office, He will show up every time, right on time.

Delivering our faith will require a new set of keys to help change our behavior towards God's will. These keys to faith will parallel the methods we use to drop of our mail because we understand that process and can transfer it to our prayer life. When we use our faith by presenting our prayers to God, with thanksgiving, without fear, and in every situation, He will act on our requests (1 John 5:14-15).

Keys to Delivering Our Faith to God

- Drop it Off
- Let it Go

Drop it Off

Before we can believe in the mailman to get our letter where we need it to go, we must first get him the letter. To drop off our mail, we need to get in the car, drive to the post office, pick a number, wait in line, and tell them what we needed, pay for stamps, drop it off, and then leave. God made it much simpler to drop off our mail, or our problems, to Him. God gave us prayer.

If we aren't talking to God about where our mail (problems) needs to go, how can He help us? Yes, the Bible says God knows what we need before we ask for it, but in the next verse, Jesus tells us to pray about those needs (Matt. 6:8-9). Jesus taught us that prayer helps us with our problems.

The first key to delivering our faith is to drop it off, which we do by going to God in prayer and asking Him to solve our problems. If we don't believe we have a solution for our problems, it is only because we didn't ask God for one in faith (James 4:2). God is the Lord over our lives, not this planet, but to get Him moving over our lives, we need to give Him permission, and we can only do that through prayer.

Faith cannot be answered without prayer because true faith in God can't be started without prayer. If we aren't praying to God for help, then we don't trust Him to take care of it. If we aren't trusting in God to take care of our problems, we are trusting in ourselves or someone else instead. Doing things that way is the equivalent of actually trying to get all those letters to all those different cities all by ourselves.

When we drop off our problems with God through prayer, He immediately begins to move on them. Clearing the path ahead, waiting in traffic, or calling others to help. It is God's job to deliver us out of our problems once we believe He will, just like any father would for his child. Our problems will be delivered no matter how hot, rainy, or icy it is. God can deliver our boss a peace to stop yelling at us, give us grace to fight off our addiction, or send someone to be a help to our life when we need it. However, the answer to our problems won't be delivered until we drop them off with God through prayer, and that prayer is evidence we have found faith in Him.

Challenge:

> Drop off your prayers right now. Activate the work of the God (postman) in your life by delivering your letters (problems) in the blue bins (prayers). Ask God to then turn off your worry for all that is on your mind and *know* that your faith will allow God to finally give you an answer to that problem.

> The unofficial post office motto is as follows: "Neither snow nor rain nor heat nor gloom of night stays these couriers from the swift completion of their appointed rounds." Our faith is secure in the post office to follow through with that. Do you want to be someone that has more faith in the post office than in God? Stop reading this for a moment and pray. Ask God for help; believe it will come. Know God's future for your life is better than your past.

Let it Go

The key to letting our letters (problems) go is to stop worrying about them, or be at rest, after they are delivered to the Postman (God) in the blue bins (prayer). We let go of our worry when we do not double check on God's work by continually asking Him to solve the same prayer. God does

not need us to pray excessively to move in our lives, just to pray faithfully.

When we make a checklist of things we need to get done, like get groceries, gas, and go to post office, we don't finish those errands, and then double check to make sure they're done. We wouldn't call the post office to remind them to deliver our package, yet when we pray, we keep going back to God to remind Him about our prayer.

When we make checklists, we cross things off of them when we finish. Jesus has already finished all the work God gave Him to do on our behalf (John 17:4). Jesus has already checked everything off of our lists, so when we go to Him in prayer all we have to do is accept the finished work of Jesus by using our faith to believe the answer to our prayer will arrive.

Letting go is the luxury that our faith in Christ gives us. Jesus made a sacrifice at the cross that covered all of our sins, our mistakes, our works, our stress, our problems, our fears, and our doubts. Those debts have been paid, and Jesus covered them all. Jesus allowed us the rest that comes with doing all that work, and all we have to do is find faith in God's will for our lives to receive it.

What do we usually do after a long day of errand running after we cross everything off our list? We take a break. We relax. We sit down and unwind for a second. We *rest*.

> *"My Father has entrusted everything to me. No one truly knows the Son except the Father, and no one truly knows the Father except the Son and those to whom the Son chooses to reveal him." Then Jesus said, "Come to me, all of you who are weary and carry heavy burdens, and I will give you rest."* **Matthew 11:27–28 (NLT)**

This scripture tells us that Jesus will give rest to all who trust in Him and lay down their burdens. When we let go of our heavy burdens through prayer, Jesus will pick them up and deliver us from them. Rest is the evidence that our faith in God is working.

How do we rest? We are at real rest when we first stop worrying about whatever troubles us, and second, when we are able to start thanking God for solutions. When we deliver (prayer) our letters (problems) to God, we should be immediately at rest in our minds because after we deliver our prayers we need to begin to thank God for answering them.

Faith is what allows God to work properly in our lives, but thanking God puts our faith to work. Thanking God also puts us at rest because we know He is just helping us out of love. Our joy is present when we are at rest, and we are at rest when we thank Him.

Challenge:

Change your prayers from petition to thankfulness. When you dropped off your prayer a minute ago, you may have said, "God, please help me. I can't pay my rent," "God please help me overcome my sickness," or "God, I don't know why it's so hard for me to stop." Now, in order to get your mind at rest, we need to move on to being thankful. Change your prayer of petition (asking Him for something) to faithful delivery (thanking Him for what hasn't arrived but you believe will).

You do that by thanking God in your prayers for what He has done in your life, even before it has actually arrived. When you are behaving this way, you are in the middle of watching your faith in God's will at work. Turn your prayer life into thanksgiving with prayers like, "Thank you God for paying my rent," "Thank you for healing me," or "Thank you for grace to beat this problem I can't beat on my own." After we give our problems to God and place our faith in is His will, He will be our deliverer (Ps. 18:2).

Part Six:
Finding Faith to Overcome

Overcoming the Past

"This means that anyone who belongs to Christ has become a new person. The old life is gone; a new life has begun!" **2 Corinthians 5:17 (NLT)**

Have you ever heard someone say they received a promotion at work but then complain about it because the raise wasn't sufficient? What about someone with a new car who complained about how it got dirty the next day?

These comments come out of the hearts of people who can't overcome their pasts. When we say negative things about blessings from God, it is because we lack a faithful heart to believe our future is good. Instead, we tear down our blessings by telling others why what we have isn't good enough or why we deserve better.

Trying to overcome our past can be very difficult even for believers. Believers often compare the results of blessings we received against what we expected God to provide for us. We become disheartened when our expectations don't meet our results.

2 Corinthians 5:17 tells us that when we become born again, all things become new and that includes our life from this moment forward. Our past, and its results, no longer define us. Once we fill our hearts with Christ, we have been forgiven of our sins, and there is no more record in Heaven of our wrongs (Isa. 43:25). However, on earth we often struggle with letting go of our past results, and that attitude keeps us from the future God has for us.

Instead of focusing on our future, and faithfully believing it will get better, we often focus on the mistakes, troubles, and problems of our past. We blame our past for being the cause of our current sufferings and circumstances, or we can't see our future because we are so rooted in the life our sin nature built for us. We stay where we are in our lives of addiction, failure, and doubt because we are unable to let Jesus take those struggles from our lives.

If we are struggling to overcome situations that have already happened, it is because we are lacking the faith to remember that Jesus took all our sins, failures, and troubles of our past and erased them from our lives. All we need to do is get our minds in a new place, and remember that our past does not define our future.

To find faith in God to overcome our past, we will first need to declare our life is not what it seems, but is what God says it will be. We can declare our predetermined victory because we know the great work Christ did to erase our past sins on the cross. Christ came to remove us from our past and offer the choice of taking the path of God's will for our lives. Changing our thinking and behavior to follow Christ will allow us to accept the peace and joy that come from making that decision (1 John 4:4).

We need to spend less time getting stuck thinking about our failures and more time trying to create positive uplifting memories in our future. We need to change the narrative we use when describing our circumstances. For instance, it's a lot more common to hear someone complain about why they don't have a job than it is to hear that person talk about all the work they are doing to get one. We need to stop complaining about our past and change our tone to promote our future in God's will.

Our pasts are difficult to overcome because we like to stay defeated. It is a lot easier to mope about our problems, than it is to do what God wants us to do about them—which is to overcome them by finding faith for His will to be done our lives.

Feeling defeated is an attack of the enemy designed to foul and discredit God's promise to us of a better future that comes through faith (Heb. 11:1). Those moments when we are feeling bad, worn down, and don't want to get up in the morning are what some of the fiery arrows of the enemy look like. We are constantly under attack, and sometimes it's just as easy for the devil to defeat us by making us lazy as it is to attack us with loss, doubt, and grief. The only way to fight those battles is with faith.

However, we *know* that God answers prayer in unexpected ways, so we shouldn't be discouraged when it doesn't turn out exactly like *we* thought it should. Sometimes, it takes a lot faith to not be discouraged, but we cannot get stuck in the past by believing God can't improve our circumstances just because He didn't answer our past prayers the way *we* wanted.

We need to remember that our expectations will hardly ever match up with how God responds to our faith. In other words, God will hardly ever answer our prayers how we think He should because God will answer prayers the way He needs to. However, the struggles of our past will lead to us second guessing, and giving our negative "notes" on God's answers. This happens a lot in prayer, and we are all susceptible to it.

The best way to understand how we second guess God is when we pray a prayer that starts with the word *why*. We ask God, "Why is this happening to us," 'Why didn't I get it," or "Why can't I?" We constantly second guess God's work in our lives and the lives of others. Sharing our frustrations are incorrect ways to appreciate God's work for us. If we are responding to God with *why* prayers, they will always be prayers dealing with what happened in the past. Our faith should always be forward focused.

2 Corinthians 5:17 tells us there is no more need to look behind in our lives. We are new creations who can use faith to see an abundant future. The only important event that happened in our past is what Jesus did on the cross. Our sins are covered by grace, and there is nothing we've done, or will do, that will keep Christ from loving us. Our future is secure in the work of Christ at the cross. No past is too broken, no addiction is too powerful, and no enemy is too strong to defeat the love of Christ, and prevent Him from saving His people and bringing them into a better future.

When we stay focused on Christ, and not our circumstances, we will find victory over our past. However, we will need to find faith in God's plan for our lives to overcome our past, and we will do that by keeping our thoughts focused on our future. In turn, our behavior will change toward the directions of our thoughts. Our behavior will move us towards the future of our lives and away from our past mistakes.

To get to our new future inside God's will we need to get a new set of keys to use specifically to overcome our past with our faith. Below are the practical applications that separate us from our pasts and attach us to our new future.

Keys to Keep Focused on the Future

- **Stop Trying to Fix Our Problems**
- **Picture Our Ocean of Blessings**
- **Forgive Ourselves**

Stop Trying to Fix Our Problems

One of our biggest struggles when trying to overcome our past is trying to solve problems on our own. That is no reliance on faith in God. Our life is a reflection of what we focus on, and if we focus on fixing our past problems, our life will become troubled because only Christ provides the right fix for our broken lives. If we focus on Christ and remember that He removed poverty, sickness, and death from our lives, we won't need to fix our problems because our faith *knows* He already defeated them.

Thinking and worrying about problems all the time is a meal for doubt. Negative thoughts feed our doubt and make our doubts grow, and once it gets too heavy those doubts will be unbearable to move out of our minds. At that point, it will become hard to see around our problems and get our focus back on the abundant future God has for our lives.

The first key we acquire that will allow us to stop fixing our problems comes from a promise in God's Word:

"Commit everything you do to the Lord. Trust Him, and He will help you." **Psalm 37:5 (NLT)**

The key to giving everything to God is to commit all our actions to Him, and we do that by not trying to do things our own way. When we have the faith to trust God to do it His way, the Bible promises us God *will* help.

We must commit our ways to the Lord by stopping the bad habit of sharing our struggles with people first and God second. When trouble comes we should call God first before we call our spouse, parents, or friends. Our friends and families cannot deliver us from our afflictions, but when we go to them before God, we are giving them the first opportunities to help solve our problems. We need to stop that behavior and go tell Jesus what we are trying to overcome and be reminded in that prayer that no weapon formed against us can defeat us (Isa. 54:17).

Another thing we can do to give up our old ways of doing things is to relax when trouble comes. We can do that by spending some time in prayer upon trouble's arrival. Use that time to ask God for help. God has a cleanup crew for problems that is better than the best pit crew team on a motor speedway track. God knows how to provide peace, answers, and opportunity to fix any mess. Trying to fix our own problems puts our faith on our own abilities, and those methods are usually what get us in trouble in the first place.

> *"For there is a proper time and procedure for every delight,*
> *though a man's trouble is heavy upon him. If no one knows*
> *what will happen, who can tell him when it will happen?"*
> **Ecclesiastes 8:6-7 (NAS)**

This verse reminds us the troubles of our past burden our heart. We struggle with our future because we can't see what coming. When we try and plan out our future, we will find our solutions for problems, no matter how well thought out or perfect they seem to us, are just not right because they aren't from God.

Our ideas don't take into account the future because we haven't seen it yet. God has seen our future, and He *knows* what lies ahead of us. That is why God's ways will always be better than our ways. God knowingly steers us clear of dangers we cannot see and towards opportunities we have yet to receive. God's Word also says in this verse that doing things in the proper time will bring us delight. Doing things in the proper time is another way of saying doing things the Lord planned out or acting in the will of the God. Doing things on God's time table, and in His will, is only possible to those that find faith.

Picture Our Ocean of Blessings

The blessings we receive from our faith works just like a large flowing body of water. A tributary flows to rivers, and rivers flow toward the ocean. Each one is bigger than the last, but they all contain the same water.

Another key to use so that we can stand in faith is to picture our ocean of blessings. To overcome our past we will need to see the whole picture of God's will being done in our lives, and not just a snapshot of our present circumstances caused by the enemy. God has a future and hope planned out for us, but it will only occur one blessing at a time (Jer. 29:11).

We can overcome our past by remembering that everything God does for us is moving our life towards the goal of eventually having an ocean of blessings. Our little blessings feed our bigger blessings, and they all end up as a whole in our ocean of blessings. In other words, our ocean of blessings is the whole of our testimony of God's work in our life. To overcome our past through our actions we need to be sharing the testimony of God's future work in our lives, and not complaining about the trouble the enemy has put us in.

To overcome our past we need to stop complaining about the parts of blessings that didn't arrive. We need to stop sharing a negative testimony when the raise we received wasn't as big as we hoped, or because our spouse isn't exactly what we pictured. We need to be thankful that we received those things to begin with, no matter if the blessing was small or large, because those blessings add up.

When we declare what we think should have happened in our lives we are letting God, and others, know that we want everything *our* way. When we end up being upset because our raise wasn't big enough, it means we think we should understand why He did it that way. However, God may not have given us a bigger raise because we wouldn't steward the money wisely, and He is trying to test our spending in order to give us a way bigger raise in the future. Maybe it's possible that lack of raise sparks our interest in another line of work that God wants us to go into down the road. There are endless reasons God does things the way He does in our lives, but it's not for us to question our blessings with a bad attitude.

Our future cannot be completed without all the small and medium sized blessings that flow into our ocean of blessings. We get hung up on our past because we want all our blessings now, and our past reminds us we don't have them. Our blessings will all eventually end up in our lives, but sometimes, it takes a long time for all of them to meet up from the small places they start. We shouldn't complain, or need to find understanding, if a blessing doesn't arrive how we think it should. Instead, we should find comfort in knowing all of our blessings will end up in an ocean full of blessings, and we can fish our testimonies out of that ocean and share them with others.

Forgive Ourselves

Testimony

There would be many times in my past I would gamble away my rent money and kick myself for weeks until the day it was due. Then, finally, right before it was actually due, I would tell my roommate or someone about it who could help me. This is the most common response I received. "Why didn't you tell me sooner? It would've been easier for me to help if you would've told me before now!"

If I hadn't been so worried about being judged by them for losing the money or mad at myself for messing up again, I could've gone to them sooner. They could've helped me sooner. I prevented blessings while I pouted and waited for a miracle to come. A miracle I had no faith in God to provide.

We will always take longer to ask for help than God will take to provide it. Messing up and feeling badly are parts of life, but God has plans to turn our lives around. We will constantly fall, but believers are supposed to get back up and fight the good fight of faith (Prov. 24:16).

The Lord's Prayer asks God to forgive us of our sins as we forgive others who have sinned against us. Do we pray that prayer and think about forgiving ourselves?

People who can't forgive themselves, and don't know where they are going are never going to overcome their past. However, people in faith *know* where they are going and have no need to look back.

The last key we can use to overcome our past is to forgive ourselves. Our faith in God cannot move forward while we feel sorry for ourselves or mad about the events of our past. God does not want us to punish ourselves for our mistakes either. Christ took all of our punishment at the cross, and as believers, we are no longer going to be punished for our sins, and we shouldn't punish ourselves either (1 John 1:9).

We forgive ourselves through the knowledge of our sins being forgiven at the cross, but our behavior must follow our change in thinking. We know we have forgiven ourselves when we stop crying about our past. It is okay to grieve, but the loss or struggles existing in our pasts are to be given to God, so that He can give us peace, joy, and deliverance from those things.

God loves us and will help us overcome our pasts, but God is *only* moved by faith in Him. God is not moved to help us when we pout, complain, or cry because those aren't actions of faithful believers. It is okay to cry, and God will often comfort us when we cry. However, God doesn't help us just because we started crying; instead, He runs to help us because we asked for help while we were crying.

Another way we forgive ourselves is to stop feeling sorry for ourselves. This behavior is often called throwing a pity party, and while we are throwing them, we don't ask God for help. No one likes to get help when they feel frustrated by life's events. Sulking, questioning, and feeling depressed will feed our sin nature's hunger that we deserve to get our way in life.

God has a better future planned for our lives, but when we doubt our future in His will because we can't overcome the past, the future fails to manifest. When we spend time feeling sorry for ourselves, we are limiting our relationship with God. We aren't going to God during our pity parties because if we were, God would bless us with peace and joy to know our circumstances won't last.

We should be claiming the victory God has promised us over our past and finding faith to look forward to our future filled with God's promises.

As a believer, Christ covers us. Our sins are covered, our judgment is covered, and our punishment is covered. We can't be afraid to confess our problems and ask for help. God already knows and has already answered them through Jesus at the cross. When we ask for help, it means we *know* we messed up, and we *know* we can't do it our way anymore. The relief and that feeling of weight being lifted off of our shoulders is evidence of our faith in God at work.

Overcoming Doubt

"Then Jesus said to the disciples, "Have faith in God. I
tell you the truth, you can say to this mountain, 'May you
be lifted up and thrown into the sea,' and it will happen.
But you must really believe it will happen and have no
doubt in your heart. I tell you, you can pray for anything,
and if you believe that you've received it, it will be yours."
Mark 11:22–24 (NLT)

In these verses, Jesus tells us to have faith in God. Jesus tells us that faith is achieved, when we have no doubt in our heart. Jesus tells us that our faith can accomplish things that seem impossible, and that faithful prayers will be answered, but Jesus does not tell us how to overcome doubt. We need to learn how to overcome doubt and understand that even a small amount of it can cause our lives trouble.

Picture you have swept the floor in your kitchen. You take the broom and sweep from one side and then move to another pushing dirt in many different directions yet making one pile. Imagine that you now you have all the dirt and random pieces of trash piled in the center of the room. You move to pick up the big stuff on the top of the pile and toss it in the trash. After that, you get the dust pan, and sweep as much of the pile into it, and then empty the dust pan in the trash. After several passes, you are left with that pesky line of dirt that doesn't get swept into the dustpan. What do you do with that last line of very tiny, but noticeable dirt?

Do you consider yourself finished sweeping? Would you sweep it under the fridge, get a towel and wipe it up, or vacuum it up?

Does it bother you that it doesn't just come up the first time? Is it frustrating when you have to take all those extra steps to remove such a little line of dirt?

When that line is left on the floor in your kitchen would you tell anyone that your floor was clean? What if you just filled up two trash bags, but there is still that little line left. Is it completely clean?

Doubt in our lives is like that pesky little line of dirt on our kitchen floor. How God deals with our life is also very similar to how we sweep up our kitchen. When God is sweeping up our life, He pushes us in one direction and then pushes us in another. God gets our life piled up right where He wants it, and the He begins to clean up our lives.

First, God bends over to pick up our big problems and put them in the trash. God wants to takes away the addictions, the abuse, a bad home life, or money problems, before He works on removing anything else. After God is finished with the big things, He is left with a pile that is *already* a lot smaller.

God then goes to the closet, gets His dustpan out, and sweeps up the medium sized struggles next. God works to remove the problems like money for bills, scheduling problems, and arguments with friends or family. God can easily push those problems into the dust pan and throw them away. God might take several passes through our lives, just to make sure He got all the medium and small problems. Small problems could include, but aren't limited to, healing a broken friendship, putting gas in our car, or giving us an idea for that difficult new project at work.

Our faith in God should allow us to let Him do all the work in our life, just like we let our broom do all the work in the kitchen. When God is finished cleaning up our problems, He looks down and sees that pesky line of doubt still in our lives. When we doubt God, we are actually putting faith on our own abilities, thoughts, actions, and words. Our doubt leaves behind a tiny line of dirt for God to pick up from our lives. That tiny line prevents God from giving our life a complete clean.

Finding faith in God to overcome our doubts starts by realizing how easy it is for God to help us. God sees our

problems, like we see a pile of dirt when we have a broom. There is minimal effort, if any, for God to remove our problems. We then need to understand that God will deliver us from all our problems, big and small, and our doubt, when we find faith to rely on Him, instead of ourselves (Ps. 54:7).

In order for God to finish cleaning our lives, we must first allow our faith to eliminate doubt. Doubt puts a halt to the whole process of God's work in our life, and unfortunately, this will be a lifelong work. Our kitchen floors don't stay clean forever and will require us to sweep them again. Our lives are no different, and even after God removes our dirt, we will begin to create a new pile of sins that He will need to pick up later. The only way we can let God do a deep clean on our lives from time to time is by overcoming doubt.

Doubt allows our lives to stay complicated and leaves us feeling unclean. Once God starts moving to clean our lives, He does all the work. Our faith, and His grace, will get all the big debris put away first. Then, our faith will allow God to work on the medium and small problems, and it takes a few passes, but He will eventually take care of it. However, there are always problems we aren't giving to God. There is always a little doubt left behind somewhere.

Our doubt sometimes leaves a line of problems that we make it harder for God to pick up. We find it easy to give God some troubles in our lives, but problems that are too big, too hard, or need supernatural faith are difficult to rely on God's help to find victory. Our doubt still remains in those places where we aren't giving all our troubles to God.

Our doubt for a situation will usually begin to grow because we can't grasp an understanding of how God will fix whatever the problem is. Doubt is what ultimately slows down, limits, and prevents our faith from working to see God's will done in our lives. In the spectrum of things, the tiny line we see in our kitchen is how God sees the doubt in our lives. Doubt is a bit of an inconvenience, but it's still easy to overcome.

We need keys to unlock our thinking to allow doubt to be swept out of our minds. These keys to removing doubt will highlight the expectations we need to hold in our hearts. When we are full of expectation and understand our need to persevere, our faith in God will attack and destroy the doubt in our minds. When we walk with these keys, our floors will stay dirt free, and the Holy Spirit will continually remind us to ask God for help cleaning up the mess in our lives.

Keys to Removing Doubt

- **Hope**
- **Perseverance**

Hope

Hope is a precious commodity, and most people would say they desire to have it. However, true hope is only attained through faith in God, and most people struggle finding faith in Him. They struggle because faith happens when believing for the better future God's will for our lives promises, and many of us can't see past the problems we are currently facing. Hope is a byproduct of faith. When we see the future God has planned for us as bright, hope will then overflow in our hearts.

Has your life been as you hoped for thus far? Is there something you wish you could change? What about something you would get if you had a wish? Do you hope for more money, a better house, a bigger family, a spouse, a job you enjoy, or maybe just a vacation?

Having hope is possible because of all the promises God made us in the Bible. However, if we don't know what God promises us, the hope that we gain through faith in those promises will diminish. God wants us to have an abundant life full of all our heart desires (Ps. 37:4). God loves us, and God's love is a giving love. God wants to give us a satisfying life.

Do you feel like you are living a satisfying life? If not, you can ask God for one. He can fill your life with hope. Hope is a promise from God.

> *"I pray that God, the source of hope, will fill you completely with joy and peace because you trust in him. Then you will overflow with confident hope through the power of the Holy Spirit."* **Romans 15:13 (NLT)**

God wants our lives to *overflow* with hope. God is the source of hope. Our faith in God overcomes doubt because He provides us with abundant hope. God provides us with more than we could ever ask or think because He loves us (Eph. 3:20). However, without an understanding of how the love of Christ works, we are never going to be full of hope, but rather suffering, misunderstanding, and a hole in our hearts that will never be filled.

The key to overcoming doubt is gained by understanding how the love of Christ works. Christ showed His love when He came to Earth and died for our better future. Our faith needs to cling to that better future Christ died to give us. Christ's love is giving, and giving life is the ultimate evidence of love. To overcome doubt, we must believe our lives can get better by establishing a relationship with Jesus Christ as our Lord and Savior.

Christ always has more for us. We must have hope for our future. Many people live happily and feel blessed, but there is more to what Christ has for us. There is even more satisfaction we can receive in our lives when we use our faith to follow Christ down the path God laid out for us to take.

First, when we allow God to take over our direction, even though we won't acquire all He wants for us overnight, we will get abundant hope. Faith means *knowing* what we ask for will arrive. Faith doesn't mean we are lucky. Luck is not real thing. However, faith and hope are very real.

There is no real reason to believe our future can't be better. God wants to give us hope. We need to say we have hope, declare it, and tell others how God is in complete control of our lives, and we are not filled with doubt. We need to trust in God and thank Him for our abundant future, and then we will be blessed by God with increased hope (Jer. 17:7). We overcome when our hope increases because it leaves less room for doubt.

Perseverance

We can't live a life without getting knocked down (Prov. 24:16). The enemy comes only to steal, kill, and destroy our life (John 10:10). In order to live hopefully and faithfully, we must overcome doubt through perseverance. We persevere when we continue to get back up each time the enemy knocks us down. We may fall seven times, but faithful people need to get up eight times (Prov. 24:16).

The greatest stories we will ever hear are ones of perseverance. We find them in real life and at the movies. Movies almost always see the hero run into some sort of difficulty only to overcome it later and find victory in the end. The Bible says we are overcomers, and we can claim victory over adversity just like the heroes at the movies we go and see (1 John 5:4). Lives of faith are just reflections of those films we watch, where we see a good guy fight and get knocked down, only to get up and defeat the enemy in the end.

The key to overcoming and finding faith in God to persevere is to be people that get back up when life knocks us down. When we don't stay down, defeated, and full of doubts we believe God's future plans for us are better than our circumstances. Getting up after being knocked down is evidence of faith.

Believers know their lives will be full of trouble, but we know we have the shield of faith to protect us. When we use that shield to deflect arrows, we will find it easier to get back up because we won't be so hurt from a direct hit. The more often we get back up, the more testimonies of perseverance our lives will create. When we share those testimonies, we will leave behind a trail of evidence that says we have overcome doubt, and *know* how to find faith in God.

Testimony

One day when I was in my early twenties, I was flipping through channels and landed on an interview story show. The highlighted story of that show impacted my life. It was the testimony of Josh Hamilton.

Josh Hamilton is a professional baseball player. Josh was the MLB number one draft pick in 1999 and signed a several million-dollar bonus before he was nineteen. Josh was a millionaire before he ever played one game professionally. Josh grew up in a loving Christian home, and by his own account, he was loved and nurtured. However, when Josh went away to play baseball, he became addicted to drugs.

Once addicted, Josh spent the next couple years going through his millions and then some on drugs. Josh eventually failed MLB drug tests and was banned for over a year from major league baseball. Many thought that Josh would never play baseball again, and it would be just another tragic case of drugs taking another promising life.

Instead, Josh found hope in Christ and had faith that his future would get better following God's will for his life. Josh began to let God take care of all that debris and trash in his life. It didn't happen overnight, but through hard work, determination, and perseverance, Josh knew he would make it back to professional baseball. He did.

Josh eventually signed a small contract for a part time role with the Cincinnati Reds. He played hard and used his faith to overcome doubt, and God led him to victory. Josh was later traded to the Texas Rangers, and in 2008, almost a decade since his collapse, Josh hit twenty-eight homeruns in the Home Run Derby on national television for all to see. Josh was the AL MVP in 2010, and in 2013 signed a five year $125 million contract with the Los Angeles Angels. Josh gives God all the glory for his perseverance.

Josh's story of perseverance uplifted me. When I heard his story for the first time, I was in the middle of battling my own severe gambling addiction. I could relate to all that he went through. I saw how miserable Josh said he had been at the bottom of his drug addiction. At the time I was watching, I was having the same feelings he was describing God took away from him. I had problems with my family like he said he had. I also found find myself selling things that were important to me just for a high, in my case, the high that I felt gambling. I was having thoughts that my life would never get better, but God showed me the testimony of someone who overcame those same doubts. God used Josh's story to give me hope.

I carried Josh's testimony with me from the moment I heard it. I told his story to all my friends and family about what he overcame. I became Josh Hamilton's number one fan. I bought his jerseys and made my favorite team the Texas Rangers, but this was all before I was born again.

At first, I didn't realize I liked his story because Josh found faith in God. I liked it because he overcame something that was similar to what I was going through and that gave me hope to think my situation could also change. The truth is that God, through Josh's story, gave me faith to believe that God had a hope and a future for my life that didn't match my circumstances.

My faith in God didn't change as soon as I heard that story, but it planted a seed. Almost a decade had passed after I saw that story for the first time that I found Christ and put Him in charge of my life. It was only after giving my life to Christ I was able to watch as God swept my life clean, removing my biggest struggle. My former life was cluttered with so much debris, but God picked much of it up and threw it away.

Perseverance destroys doubts and provides hope. What if Josh had given up? There would be no twenty-eight HRs, an AL MVP, or two World Series appearances. What if I had given up? I would have no salvation, no future, no friends, no book, and no ministry.

God is the source of hope that provides the determination needed to fuel our drive to get up and persevere. God supplies that hope, but we need to ask Him for it. The day I finally had enough of my life, I broke down, and basically said, "God, if you're up there, I need some hope because I can't live like this anymore."

I didn't even understand what that meant exactly when I said it. I just knew I couldn't do it anymore. I needed help. My faith found Christ at the moment I knew I needed Him. I didn't find salvation just because I knew He existed, but because I knew the joy in my life was lacking. Christ supplies the joy, just like He did for me, Josh and every other believer, when we supply the faith in Him.

Overcoming Adversity

"We can rejoice, too, when we run into problems and trials, for we know that they help us develop endurance."
Romans 5:3 (NLT)

The Word of God says man was born into trouble (Job 5:7). The fiery arrows will never cease in their attacks on us, and we are not to be surprised by these attacks (1 Peter 4:12). We will always have the need to overcome adversity. We will need to *learn* to be overcomers.

We already learned why we are under attack, and we also learned that Jesus came to overcome the world so that we could as well. We now need to learn what we can do as believers to overcome adversity. This chapter contains the practical application of things we can remember and things we can do to overcome any of the trouble that finds us.

Finding faith for God's will to help us overcome adversity is more than just asking for a solution to our problems. Being able to overcome is about living in a mindset of victory that Jesus has asked us to take while facing trials. Romans 5:3 says we are to rejoice when trouble finds us. The Bible also says the men who endure their trials are blessed (James 1:12).

If we are constantly under attack and every day brings new problems to face, how are we supposed to be joyful and blessed? We will be blessed because God also promises victory over our troubles. Jesus promised us that we can overcome:

> *"I have told you all this so that you may have peace in
> me. Here on earth you will have many trials and sorrows.
> But take heart, because I have overcome the world."*
> **John 16:33 (NLT)**

Jesus was, and is, aware of our upcoming struggles. Jesus asked us to take heart in knowing that He has already overcome the world. Every problem ever faced by man was faced by Jesus. He conquered them all, and before Jesus left the disciples, He left them with this message of courage.

Overcoming adversity of any kind will not happen without faith in God's will to be done in our lives. Faith is the key that allows God to open doors, unlock opportunities, and blessings. Without faith, we will fall victim to our troubles. We need to learn how to live faithfully by applying the teachings of God's Word to our everyday lives.

The following are keys to understanding trouble, and the practical ways we can use to deal with adversity. Implementing these methods can help us to reduce, and eventually remove, complaining, and questioning from our mouths when trouble finds us. If we can remove those two things from our thoughts and speech we will be exhibiting the peace that Jesus came to bring us. We will then be able to call it all joy *and* be blessed by our troubles.

We need to stay standing in our battles against the enemy long enough to see God's victory arrive. Paul tells us in Romans 5:3 when we face trials we will grow in endurance. With that promise, we can find joy in knowing that trials will come, but we will develop the strength to knock each one down.

Keys to Overcoming Adversity

- **Realize Trouble Finds Us Everyday**
- **Laugh and Count it All Joy**
- **Speak Scripture**
- **Be Quick to Listen and Slow to Speak**

Realize Trouble Finds Us Everyday

Being equipped with the knowledge that trouble finds us every day and also understanding that some days are just worse than others is essential when dealing with adversity. Knowing that trouble comes every day prevents us from thinking we are being singled out. Faith in Christ provides relief from attacks and persecutions, but it does *not* completely stop them.

One solution to handling our bad days is to not complain about them to others or question why God would do this to us. We need to realize that the troubles we are facing today are no different than the problems of any other day. God has a plan of getting us through them and limiting the severity of today's problems. We must recognize all problems are solvable by God.

If trouble comes at us every day, we should realize that our troubles aren't as life altering as we sometimes make them out to be. We overuse phrases like, "My life's over," "I just can't handle this right now," or "This is the worst thing that could happen!" Attacks are all designed with the purpose of instilling doubt in our minds in order to keep us away from God. These types of phrases stir up our doubt and suppress our faith.

The key to using our faith in God to overcome adversity is to not speak or behave differently based on the size of our troubles. Problems, regardless of size, are just an attack, and big problems aren't any harder to overcome than small ones because we use the same faith to overcome them all! If faith the size of a mustard seed moves mountains, a tiny amount of faith is more than enough to get us through whatever we are going through today (Matt. 17:20).

The sooner we give God control of our situation, the faster He will handle it. We give God control when we begin to consciously realize that this moment we are facing isn't the worst thing on earth and turn our focus on God to bring a solution instead of worry. We do that through prayer and positive words.

Our words are the first way that faith and doubt happen. We shouldn't use overused phrases to describe how bad our lives are to others. To overcome adversity, our testimonies need to be positive and uplifting. Remember, if we are facing trouble we need to announce that God has it under control.

Next, we need to understand that every problem we are facing has the same solution. The solution to our problems is to give them to God in prayer. Prayer activates our faith by accepting the peace Jesus promised and allowing Him to relieve us of our worries.

Challenge:

1) Discredit trouble. When you are faced with adversity, take time to downplay the situation. Jesus conquered death, and He said we are more than conquerors (Rom. 8:37). Since you are a conqueror through Christ, you can certainly see your problems at home, work, or in your relationships defeated.

   No problem gets solved in God's will without faith, and faith is activated through prayer. Use your mouth to discredit what the enemy is trying to get you to believe. He wants you to think you have no future, and your problems will overtake you. You have a shield of faith. Trouble cannot defeat you.

2) Overcome adversity by asking God to intervene on your behalf, receive the peace that comes from giving your problems to God. Finally, remember to endure by getting up when you get knocked down. Don't let your problems keep you on the couch, or in bed. Keep moving forward with your life. We need to build our endurance because we need to be standing as long as we can for God's answer to arrive. Don't give up believing Jesus will arrive with an answer; He will.

Laugh and Count it All Joy

When we stub our toes or bang our heads, we are often heard shouting words that aren't in faith. It is our normal reaction to take pain or news that causes pain badly. Our first instinct when trouble comes is usually to shout, get angry, or wish it didn't happen.

We will always struggle with having negative reactions first because God gave us emotions, but knowing that the words we are using carry great power will hopefully persuade us from relying on the instincts of our negative emotions when trouble comes. Instead, we should try to lean on positive emotions when trouble comes, so that our faith in God isn't immediately disabled.

When we are in pain we take medicine to stop it, and laughter is often called the best medicine. There is a lot of truth to that common expression. Laughter causes us to relax and brings a since of peace with it. It is very hard to laugh without peace. Maybe we should try using laughter and joy in times of pain to bring peace. Peace, after all, is what Jesus said we would have when we overcome adversity (John 16:33).

Have you ever seen a child upset over being punished or not getting his/her way, and then takes a defiant stand against their parents? The child might stomp his/her feet angrily at the situation and to remedy this, the parent might try and get him/her to laugh, and the child will have no part of it. When that child is mad there is *no way* he/she wants to laugh. The child will take a firm stance to let us know what he/she faces is a serious issue, and the child wants his/her serious feelings to be understood by others. The adult might then begin to tickle the child, and even though he/she is not happy, the child will eventually succumb to the effects of laughter brought on by tickling. Soon after, everyone begins to find joy from their laughter. The situation, while not necessarily resolved, has been brought some relief.

The key to using our faith in God to overcome adversity is to count it all joy. Laughter brings relief, decreases the severity of the situation, and allows people to be level headed when making decisions. We need to laugh in the face of

trouble, and use our laughter to grow our faith. However, not every situation is funny or appropriate to laugh, but finding ways to laugh in situations that are can bring peace to the resolution.

The first words out of our mouth, after a problem begins, are the starting blocks for how we will build the results. If our problem solving foundation is built on blocks of negative words, we will likely have to back up and start over in order to replace them. We have to do things this way so that we can do it the right way after all. When we start off doing something wrong and have to go back and start over, it will always end up taking much longer to resolve the problem then it would've taken to do it correctly from the beginning.

For example, let's say there was an accident where someone spilled red paint on the carpet of your house.

Let's look at two possible responses:

1) "I can't believe you did that; you ruined my floor, and now we'll have to stay up all night just to fix that mess!"
2) "Oh, look at that; you spilled paint on the carpet, and it got everywhere! It looks like we will have a big mess to clean up. I guess we better get started. I always wanted to see what a red carpet would look like!"

The difference in responses is clear. The problem is the exact same, but the ways to handle it are completely different. Deciding the right way to respond and following that path is important to handling adversity wisely.

Finding joy and laughter are easy ways to stay positive in tough situations. Many of us wouldn't be happy if red paint spilled on our carpet, but joking about wanting to see it as a different color is better than yelling at someone for an accidental mistake. Imagine if God yelled at us for every mistake we made!

If we just can't find a way to laugh about a situation; then, we should at least count it all joy.

"Dear brothers and sisters, when troubles come your way, consider it an opportunity for great joy. For you know that when your faith is tested, your endurance has a chance to grow. So let it grow, for when your endurance is fully developed, you will be perfect and complete, needing nothing." **James 1:2–4 (NLT)**

James 1:2–4 highlights the results of acting in faith. James tells us that we will face many troubles, and we should be excited because those troubles will give us a chance to use our faith. Our faith for God's work to be done in our lives should be increased through continued use. Joy, as we discussed throughout this book, is a result of faith. This verse acknowledges that even in trouble, joy can be present. Finally, this verse tells us that when we act in faith we will need nothing. God uses this verse to remind us that when we have faith, we will not need anything else because faith *knows* our needs will be met.

We may not be able to laugh at the death of a loved one, but we may be able to find joy in knowing they are with Jesus, or that we are able to visit with relatives we haven't seen in a while. It isn't always easy to act this way, and it usually goes against our first response of emotion, but God is our peace provider, and laughter is the easiest way to know if we have joy. Our joy is a sign that peace is upon us, and that lets us know that we have found our faith.

Challenge:

Next time you face a problem, count it all joy. Write down three positive things that can come from a negative situation. If you are laid off, you might write, "God has a better job He needs me to get," "I will have the opportunity at a new job to build relationships and share the gospel," or "My schedule has now opened up to pursue my lifelong vision." Those are all better ways of thinking to promote your attitude to joy, but they will take practice and endurance to use them consistently. However, when you do apply those methods, your faith in Christ will provide peace and joy, even in the eyes of adversity!

Speak Scripture

A key to using our faith in God to overcome adversity is to speak scripture over the situation. Jesus did this three times while He was tempted by the enemy in the wilderness. Speaking scripture needs to be our first instinct when facing a problem, and our faith in that scripture will produce God sized results.

> *"And we know that God causes everything to work together for the good of those who love God and are called according to his purpose for them."* **Romans 8:28 (NLT)**

One of the things this verse tells us is God can take a bad situation, and turn the outcome into a pleasant one. No matter what has happened to us, God has a solution that will turn our life around for the better because of it. There is no better way of recognizing a solution to our problems than to speak the Word of God over them because God's Word tells us what solution will arrive.

Romans 8:28 tells us that the solution to our troubles will always make our lives better. The solution we should be looking for in this verse is a better life, and we should eventually be able to recognize if our lives are better off after we started declaring that scripture. Any recognition of promises fulfilled can only come if we are looking for the specific promise of God that is detailed in His scriptures.

There are countless things God can do for our problems and scriptures that match up with each one of those problems. It is so important to lean on God through His Word in the Bible to get through tough times, or God's will for us to have the best possible solution may never arrive.

My gambling problem destroyed my relationships, friendships, and a decade of my life. Without that problem being turned around into good, I wouldn't be writing this, I wouldn't be in constant fellowship with other believers, and I wouldn't be walking a path designed specifically for me by God.

Not every situation turns out for good right away, and sometimes we'll never quite see what good came out of it. God protects all who are called for His purpose, even if we don't see the cliff ahead. Declaring Romans 8:28 over our lives when trouble comes will activate our faith and give power to God to act on our behalf. God will not allow us to be a victim but will instead provide victory.

Challenge:

1) Strive to make Romans 8:28 a scripture you always have in your heart. Remember it, and repeat it *often*. Let this verse be a declaration over your life. This verse reminds us that God's plan not only involves resolution of our problems but tells us that life can get *better* because of it. Imagine how strong your muscle of faith would grow if you were able to see every negative situation in your life be turned around into a positive one?

2) Recognize God's will at work in your life. Let's pretend you are trying to sell your home and look for another one. What if you watched as the house you really wanted to buy was sold to someone else. You would be upset, and suppose because you missed out on that house, you ended up selling your house for thousands more than you would've gotten for it earlier. Wouldn't you be happy? Would you be able to notice that God turned that negative situation into a positive result?

Let's say you were in a car accident that led to a test which revealed early stage cancer. You spent months in the hospital, but eventually the cancer was able to be removed before any life threatening symptoms appeared. You would be overjoyed to be cured, but how would your faith act before the cure arrived. Would you be able to see that God turned a bad situation into a positive result?

Be Quick to Listen and Slow to Speak

Our first response to trouble is so crucial to how events in our lives play out. If we are unable to laugh or remember the scriptures God has given us, then we are left with this. Don't speak. Many of us have heard the phrase, "If you don't have anything nice to say, don't say anything at all." This phrase can be applied to our faith in God as well.

There will be times our words cannot describe a positive outcome, or it looks too bleak. We may find that we are just too stubborn to reach out to God for help because we are mad our problem happened in the first place. We are born to react this way because our sin nature is angry when we can't get our way.

God does not want us to act according to our plans, but God pleasing actions don't come naturally to us, and we will need to be taught His ways in order to walk our life in His direction. We need the knowledge that God's way is at constant battle with our way of doing things. We need to understand that striving to follow Him won't always come easy.

A key to using our faith in God to overcome adversity is to be quick to listen and slow to speak. We were born with two ears and one mouth. We are designed to listen more than we talk. If we can't be positive when we face a problem, let us attack it with silence. Saying nothing doesn't disable our faith; instead, it gives us the time we need to think back to what we have learned about how God calls us to overcome adversity. Our faith is strengthened by the use of positive words first, but it is protected by silence in moments we cannot find the right words.

For most of us being quiet is associated with peace. "I just need some peace and quiet" is a common expression. Don't think of silence as halting you from your solution, but rather preventing a false start or a need to go back and start over. Peace is the resulting proof that our faith in God's will to be done is present and working in our life.

Our faith is like a balancing scale. Faith is very temperamental if there is nothing on it. The lightest weight in any direction will tip it one way or the other. On that same scale, when a lot of weight is put on one side it is firm and heavy. Our negative words are like a brick on that scale and it will take a brick of faith on the other side to equal it out again. We will need even more faith to tip the scale in the direction of God's will. If we are able to stay silent until we can be focused on God, it is like that brick was never laid down on the scale. If there isn't anything on the scale, it will only take a little bit of faith to get our faith moving towards God's plan of action.

Our faith gets lost sometimes, just like our keys, and silence is a time to walk around and look for it. Once we begin talking, we have either found it, or we are walking around without it. If we lose our keys, we wouldn't walk to the car without them, and we shouldn't talk without joy in our possession either. Whether we lost our faith in God, or our keys, sometimes being quiet until we find them is our best course of action.

Challenge:

> When you are hit with bad news for the first time, take a deep breath, and take a moment for yourself. You won't be able to remove all of those terrible thoughts from running through your mind. No amount of training will be able to remove doubtful thoughts.

> What you can train yourself to do is to be silent and make sure that whatever you decide to say first is directed towards God or is positive in response. If you can't find the words that will express those two things, stay silent. It will always be better to say nothing than disable your faith in God with words filled with doubt and anger.

Part Seven: Is Our Faith Active?

Are We Experiencing God?

> *"May you experience the love of Christ, though it is too great to understand fully. Then you will be made complete with all the fullness of life and power that comes from God."* **Ephesians 3:19 (NLT)**

Ephesians 3:19 tells us that we will be full of life and power, gifted from God, when we take time to experience love through Christ. There are a number of ways we can experience God in order to gain information and find faith for ourselves. Each one offers a different opportunity to feel the presence of God and will also put our heart in a state of worship. Worshipping God allows Him to speak His will to us in a way we can hear, understand, and experience Him.

Finding faith to experience God requires sacrifice. The time we set apart for God and the effort we make during that time leads to our experiences. We should all strive to know Christ better, and also the Holy Spirit, who is our comforter, teacher, and power (John 14:26). These sacrificial opportunities to seek out God are usually limited to our own desire to do them. However, we will find that when we sacrifice our time for the Godhead, we will experience them in our lives!

These are the keys we can use to experience God. These are God given ways to sacrifice our time to worship the Lord. All of these methods will bring us into the presence of the Lord and give us the chance to hear His voice. Listening to God will encourage our faith to grow because when God talks to us, He is directing our path. It will take faith to walk where God asks us to walk on that path. We will *know* our faith is active when we begin hearing from the Lord and then by being doers of God's will in our lives.

Keys to Experiencing God

- **Prayer**
- **Bible**
- **Church**
- **Fellowship**

Prayer

Prayer is our direct connection with God. Prayer is simply calling a friend, our best friend, to talk about what is going on in our lives. We can pray anywhere, with anyone, or by ourselves. We can pray with our eyes opened or closed. We can turn the lights on or off. We pray to get answers for life's questions, to share our requests, and also to thank God for all He does. God knows the moment when we are talking to Him, and most importantly, we don't have to be a believer for God to hear us.

Starting to pray will break down walls we have around our faith and allow it to start working properly. Faith comes from hearing the Word of God (Rom. 10:17). When we begin to pray the Words of God out loud, our faith will follow.

We can pray for whatever we want (Mark 11:24). God has the desire to answer our prayers (Ps. 37:4). God loves us so much that when He answers our prayers, He will *always* give more than He receives from us (Eph. 3:20). God wants to answer our prayers so that we can have a fulfilled life. When praying, remember that God knows what will satisfy and fulfill our lives, and it isn't always what we are asking Him for.

It's okay to pray for help for ourselves, and our families. We can pray for financial, emotional, and physical help. We should be asking God to deliver His will in our lives by providing our food, clothing, protection, cars, houses, jobs, and relationships. We can also pray to tell Christ how we're doing today, tell Him about the things that upset us, and share our joy with Him.

God has an answer for all our prayers, and our God wants to be involved in every detail of our lives. We should be going to God in every area of our lives, and asking for the things we desire. The Bible tells us we have not because we ask not (James 4:2). We just have to ask the one person who actually can provide it for us!

The idea of praying for and over everything in life leads us to one very common misconception about prayer.

God is too big and/or too busy to answer little prayers.

This is simply not true. Christ came to have a relationship with all of us. That personal relationship is the center of our faith. When we have a personal relationship with someone like a parent or significant other, don't we share most details of our lives with them? We share the details of our lives with everyone. Look at how we share our lives on social media. If we share that much of our life with others, shouldn't we include our God in it, too?

The misconception that God doesn't answer little prayers leads to a lack of prayers, and in return, a lack of answers. Our prayer life often limits God by only inviting Him into our lives when something bad has happened or when we are hoping for a miracle. God desires us to pray without ceasing because He knows He is the only One who can actually provide for us (1 Thess. 5:17).

God hears *all* prayers, and responds to them with the same level of importance. God has no system for sifting out important prayers to answer first, and there is no line for prayers to get answered in the order they are received.

Begin to have open communication with God by picking up the phone. Prayer is the only call we will ever make, that never drops out, gets disconnected, or is a wrong number. Prayer will never go to voice mail, and God will never hang up on us. As we begin to experience God through prayer, our faith in Him will instantly increase.

Bible

Another way to experience God and get first hand training from Him is to open the Bible. While reading a book isn't normally considered an experience, the Bible is completely different and stands apart from any other book we will ever read. The Bible tells us that the Word of God in the scriptures is alive, active, and able to penetrate and touch our hearts (Heb. 4:12). That sounds like an experience to me.

The Bible contains more information than we could process in many lifetimes. The Bible has never changed, yet it stays completely relevant. God's Word also shines light on situations happening today, the same as it did in the past.

As long as people have been alive, they have had the same way of thinking, acting, and behaving. Our emotions are no more advanced, or different than those experienced by people living two thousand years ago. People experienced anger, pain, loss, joy, hope, and love back then, in the same way we do today. The Bible shares stories of people experiencing God through those emotions, and we can be encouraged by their testimonies to overcome and be blessed in our lives today.

The Bible is our guidebook to life. It provides insight, information, and plenty of lessons to be learned. In fact, many believers will read through the Bible several times in a lifetime and will realize that it *always* has more information to give and that there is *always* something new God can reveal to us inside its pages.

One of the really cool ways the Bible is an experience is its use of *rhema* words. Rhema words are what God uses to speak to us as we read the Bible. Rhema is a Greek word used to differentiate the way God speaks in scripture. Rhema translates to utterance or something said.

When we are reading the Bible, we will sometimes come across a section, passage, or sentence that makes us stop in our tracks. A verse that stands out or makes us think, "That was written just for me," or "That applies to me *right now!*" This experience is not a coincidence; it is a rhema word.

When we read our Bible and experience a rhema word, we should *know* that God is using that scripture to speak to us *right now*. God uses scripture to offer insight into our lives, speak truth into our current situations, and allow us the opportunity to grow in wisdom by giving us new-found knowledge.

Testimony

One of the first times I encountered a Rhema word was while I was reading through Hebrews. I got to Hebrews chapter 11 verse 1, and my translation read:

> *"And what is Faith? Faith gives substance to our hopes, and makes us certain of realities we do not see."*
> **Hebrews 11:1 (NEB)**

At the time I got that rhema word, I was new to Christ. I was reading through the New Testament for the first time, and a lot of my questions revolved around what exactly is faith? Jesus had asked the apostles to have more of it. Jesus said we could move mountains when we used it and that it was *through faith* that we are saved (Eph. 2:8). I didn't quite understand what that meant, and then I read this verse.

All of a sudden, I understood. The answer to my prayer was written out plainly to see, and understand, as if it were written just to answer my question. That passage was engrained in me, as if I thought of it myself, or studied it my whole life. Hebrews 11:1 helped me, taught me, and gave me knowledge I didn't have a moment before. I was experiencing God!

Rhema words can come to us at any point when we read the Bible. We may see them often, or we may go a season without seeing one, either way, a rhema word is a scripture that didn't stand out to us until today. It might be a verse we never came across, or maybe it wasn't explained to us in a way we were able to understand until now.

Whatever the case, reading the Bible is a direct path to knowledge, and reading it is an experience no other book will ever provide.

Church

Everything on the earth is dying, all the people, plants, and animals will eventually die. However, the church is the only other thing on earth besides the Word of God, which scripture tells us, will last forever (Matt. 16:18; Eph. 3:20). If the church is like the Bible, in the fact that it is able to live and thrive when everything around it is dying, it sounds like a place to experience something to me.

Worshipping at church through music, prayer, study, and fellowship is an ultimate way to experience Christ, and we will be unable to get that experience anywhere else. God inhabits praise, the only way to experience God is to worship Him, and the church is normally the place where we gather to worship.

All believers should be a part of a church. Community, fellowship, teachings, and group worship are essential to the growth and development of any believer. With that being said, we don't all need to attend the same church.

We should find a church that feels like an experience to us personally. There is a church for us that plays the type of worship music we like, has a pastor we feel teaches in a way we connect with, and has a congregation of people we feel at home with. These things lead to an experience. Church should not be a chore, or something that we feel is hard to wake up and go to. Church is not a job; it is our direct connection with other believers, and the God who loves us.

Finding a church and creating a routine to be a part of that church will create an opportunity for God to pass on His wisdom and knowledge to us every week. Church should be like a show we don't want to turn off or a book we can't put down.

Salvation won't come from attending church, but it will prepare our hearts to hear from God. God wants to tell us that He loves us. God wants us to be a part of His kingdom, and He is *always* reaching out to us. Finding faith, and God, is easier when we are looking where they are found. We will find God, and faith, where there is worship, and we find worship at the local church.

Fellowship

Experiencing God isn't always as formal as going to church and can be done without opening a book or being in prayer. Thefreedictionary.com defines fellowship as the sharing of *experiences* with others. To experience God through fellowship, we should surround ourselves with friendships of other believers and spend time with them.

Spending time with believers will allow us to see things in a new perspective. Some people may have misconceptions about believers, and think that they try too hard to be right all the time. They may feel like believers live a life where someone tells them what to do. Being an unbeliever and trying to hang out with a believer can be difficult (because it was for me).

All of those feelings of disbelief, frustration, and stomach pains an unbeliever have when the subject of faith gets brought up while fellowshipping are all attacks of the enemy to get us out of that situation. Those feelings are a real life example of God's Word:

> *"All who do evil hate the light and refuse to go near it for fear their sins will be exposed."* **John 3:20**

Testimony

I went to church growing up and left the church completely as a young teenager, and I lived a life of my own devices. During that time, I found myself uncomfortable and eager to change the subject of religion or faith when my believer friends would bring it up. I would often get angry if the conversation went on too long. That is the feeling I had every time, yet I said to those friends that I believed in God and thought I was going to heaven.

How could they both be true? How can I hate the things of God and believe in them? I couldn't. I wasn't going to heaven then even though I said I was. It wasn't until I repented and believed in my heart Jesus saved me that my salvation came. I struggled to find faith for a better future through Christ, and I believed in God, so I can only imagine the struggle it must be for anyone who has a strong disbelief of God to find faith in Christ as Lord.

What I can tell you from what I've seen since my transformation into a new creation or since I have been born again is this: Christian fellowship probably isn't what you think it is.

Christian fellowship includes the same things a lot of unbelievers do. Believers watch movies and television. Christians go to coffee shops and out to dinner at the same places everyone else goes. They like to watch sports and make jokes just like "normal" people. There is not a constant conversation about God. However, they are generally thankful to God for bringing them together and aren't usually uncomfortable when the subject of Christ is discussed.

Christians talk to each other just like anyone else would. Believers have problems with the opposite sex, at work, at church, and at home, and they discuss these problems with others, just like anyone else would. The difference between how Christians deal with their problems compared to everyone else is that they are able to add God's perspective on their situations.

Many Christians are teachable or able to change their minds after learning. Believers use fellowship as a safe place to share and hear stories in order to learn from them. Believers are able to use what they've learned from God and implement those teachings to see God's will be done in their own life.

The most important thing to know is that believers make mistakes, too. We all do. The thing that stands apart about Christian fellowship, and makes it an opportunity to experience God is this:

Christians encourage one another to seek God's help on finding solutions.

When we fellowship with good friends we are able to be honest and also accepting of the opinions of others. The time we spend in fellowship is crucial for creating plans of actions for our future. There is one thing that can be said of almost all friendships and relationships.

We are influenced by what we hear. We will be just like who we hang around (Prov. 13:20).

If we want to get better, it is better to associate with people who are trying to do that for themselves too. If we want to get sober, we should hang out with sober people. If we want to be a musician, we should hang out with musicians. If we want to find faith, and experience God, we need to spend time with Christians.

Encouragement is essential to a productive life. If the people around us are telling us it's understandable to give up because it is too hard, those are not people we should be spending our time with. Even non-believers understand that perseverance is a factor to success. With the right type of fellowship, we will have people in our lives to help lift us up when we fall. It is when we get lifted up that we are closer to God, and we are then able to experience Him.

Testimony

When I was a gambler, I also worked at a casino, which didn't help my problem. It was here where I met most of my adult friends. The people who were around me in the casino were the ones I fellowshipped with the most.

During many points of my struggle with addiction, I sought council with these people. Many of them, I found out later would secretly talk about the depths of my problem with each other. I learned they didn't understand why I did what I did or why I couldn't stop gambling. Yet, my friends never told me about those thoughts, they only shared them with others. My friends responded to me by telling me:

- You don't have a problem.

- I'll loan you the money to play, just pay me back when you get paid.
- Come to my gambling party.
- Come with me on a trip to visit other casinos.
- You can't run badly forever.
- I'll extend you more credit.
- You lost all that!
- No wonder you lose; you didn't quit when you were ahead!
- I know you're good for a bet.

The list goes on, but the point is what I heard influenced me most. I was being encouraged, but not in the right direction. I was never able to see the future God had planned for me because I couldn't get past my current situation. Our faith in God should look forward and not accept circumstances, like I did for so long, but believe in the promise of a better future that comes through faith in God's will to be done in our lives.

My fellowship with unbelievers led me to believe it was okay to be depressed about my life, and that my struggles weren't actually real. I thought, just like when I was smoking, that I could stop on my own when I got older. The people I fellowshipped with knew and talked about my problems to everyone but me. I don't blame my friends for my problems because they were entirely my own. I just shared this to highlight how important it is to realize that who we hang around matters. Fellowshipping with people who encourage our future is better than spending time with those who don't.

My fellowship life differs greatly from the days of my gambling. Now, when I fall in my walk with Christ, I have people around me trying to get me to stay focused on God and not my problems. My desire is that one day I'm able to fellowship in an experiencing God way with those friends who think I went crazy or was "brain washed" when I found Jesus.

Are We Experiencing Peace?

"You will keep in perfect peace all who trust in you, all whose thoughts are fixed on you!" **Isaiah 26:3 (NLT)**

Faith doesn't come with a timer. It doesn't go off when it's done or tell you when it's ready. Faith in God is simply a belief that something that hasn't happened will happen in a way for God's will to be done. Without faith in God whatever we are facing can't end up how it's supposed to.

So how do we actually know when faith in God works? How can we tell if what we believe lines up with what is about to happen? How do we know if God is about to come through for us?

How can we tell if our faith in God is in the right place and realize what we are doing is working?

The answer to all those questions is peace.

When you are facing something difficult, is there not a war of thoughts being waged against each other in your mind? Does your mind fight between what to do and what not to do? Do you find yourself worried about all the possible negative outcomes? Does your mind never shut off and let you think about anything else?

War as defined by thefreedictionary.com is a state of conflict between groups, and peace is the opposite of war. Peace is a state of total freedom from conflict, stress, and worry. We face a war in our battle of faith for God's will to be done in our lives, and peace is our hopeful expectation in Christ.

In Isaiah 26:3, God promises peace to all who find faith in Him. When our eyes focus on God, we won't worry about our problems because we won't see them. Our faith, our thoughts, and our actions always need to be fixed on God.

Finding faith to experience God comes from the understanding that peace is a gift from God (Gal. 5:22). There is no way to earn it. Peace is given to us when we ask for it and believe we have received it. Heavenly peace is a feeling only experienced by believers because God grants it. Peace from God is the complete release of worry, and it allows us to know when our faith is in the right place.

Testimony

Before I found Christ, I spent many nights with a battle raging in my mind. However, my addiction had conquered me, and I was helpless. There were days I would gamble away more than I could payback in months of working. I often lost money I wasn't supposed to. The days after those events were the hardest for the war in my mind.

The war in my mind would begin like this. I would first spend countless hours analyzing all that went wrong. I would pace back and forth thinking so many thoughts about how I should've left the casino when I was winning. I thought about how I should've folded on the hands I lost or bet more on the hands I won. I would think back to how I should have read more about the weather at the football game before I bet the over in a snowstorm. Not one of those initial thoughts was directed at my future because I didn't feel like I had one. All I could think about was my past, and the mistakes that were in it.

After I finished analyzing everything, my mind moved on to damage control. How do I fix what I had just done? I would spend the next hours contemplating selling my possessions (if I had any left to sell), asking friends or people at work, calling my family, borrowing against my 401k, picking up extra shifts so that I could pay off my debts before anyone found out how deep my loses were. My mind was a battlefield. I was at war, and I never had peace.

During those toughest of times, I would often pray, even though I really didn't understand prayer. I did believe in a God. When I prayed, I would ask God why He let this happen to me. I would constantly blame Him. On my worst days, I would pray that God would let me fall asleep and never wake up. The thoughts and doubts were always so bad in my head. I felt so filthy and powerless and if this is how life was going to be for me, I didn't want to live it.

Sleep, as an unbeliever, was my great and only peacemaker. Before Christ and during those really tough days, sleep was my only friend. When I was asleep, it was the only time I could shut my brain off and not feel miserable. The second before I fell asleep, and the second after I woke up, my thoughts would flood into my head bringing with them with all the doubt, fear, and worry I could handle. Sleep gave me a time out from all of those horrible feelings I had while I was awake.

When I was in trouble I looked forward to sleeping, but what I really needed was the rest I would receive from heavenly peace.

Peace is hard to find sometimes, even when we know and love God. However, without faith in the future God has for us, heavenly peace is nonexistent in our lives. Unbelievers may feel like things are going well, and that they have peace, but it's likely they are only between troubles. It is also likely that the feeling someone thinks is peace will be fleeting. The peace God gives requires faith that goes beyond comprehension, and the path of an unbeliever will never stumble upon it (Phil. 4:7, Isaiah 59:8).

Great peace comes to those who love the law (Psalm 119). Right now, our law is to love God and love others (Mark 12:30-31). God tells us that to love means to give, so if we are to love God, we are to give something to Him. God wants us to give Him our worries, our doubts, our problems and our struggles (Ps. 55:22; 1 Pet. 5:7).

After we give those things to God, He will give us a freedom from that war inside our heads, and we will feel the silence of peace.

God talks to us in a whisper when we are in trouble, and it needs to be silent for a whisper to be heard (1 Kings 19:11–12). We find peace to overcome our troubles in our quiet time. One of our quiet time opportunities occur when we are giving our troubles to God through prayer.

> *"Come to me, all who labor and are heavy laden, and I will give you rest. Take my yoke upon you, and learn from me, for I am gentle and lowly in heart, and you will find rest for your souls. For my yoke is easy, and my burden is light."* **Matthew 11:28–30 (ESV)**

In the song "Silent Night," we sing the phrase "sleep in heavenly peace." If we sing to experience heavenly peace, it means there is a time we don't sleep in heavenly peace, and it is something we need God to provide. Peace can only come from God, and heavenly peace is what we should all strive to attain so that our faith will reach its maximum mountain moving ability!

How do we know if we have found peace to activate our faith?

We have found peace when we are able to focus our complete and honest attention on other things.

When we are facing a new problem, it doesn't mean the rest of the world stops for us. We will usually have to carry on our lives as normal while dealing with problems. We'll find ourselves still needing to go to school, work, church, or shopping for groceries. As the saying goes, "Life stops for no one."

How we are handling life, as it is moving, is what provides the most insight into our state of mind. Realizing how we are thinking about our troubled situation gives us the information we need to gauge our peace level. Knowing our level of peace will result in knowing if our faith for God's will to be done in our lives is active and working.

Exploring how we react to trouble and recognizing actions of unhealthy faith will allow us to change our thinking about what we are doing. It is only after we change our thinking about something that we will be able to change our behaviors.

We need to gain a new set of keys to determine if we have peace. Sometimes, it is easy to spot and understand that we aren't at peace, and other times it is subtle, and we may not notice. These keys will allow us to recognize if we have peace and also give us some instruction on how to open our hearts to receive God's heavenly peace if we don't.

These keys are the major ways we are able to determine whether or not we are exhibiting behavior of unrest or experiencing a lack of peace. Being able to focus on things, other than our problems is a sure sign that we have found peace. When we find peace, we know we have found faith in God.

Keys to Determine if We Have Peace

- **Being Constantly Preoccupied**
- **Filling Time with Busy Work**
- **Trouble Sleeping**
- **Complaining and Questioning**

Being Constantly Preoccupied

Have you ever been on an airplane and tried to use the restroom, but someone was in there already? A light would be on to let you know it is occupied. That light tells us that someone is in there, and we will have to wait because there is no room for us in there right now.

Our mind is like that airplane bathroom. Our mind is unable to allow different types of thoughts to occupy the same available space. Our mind can be full of thoughts but just not different types. When our mind has one type of thought, like doubt, it becomes occupied. When our mind is occupied with doubt, no other type of thought, like faith, will prevail.

The key to determining peace comes from an understanding that our faith in God needs to occupy all the space in our mind. When faith is working, our mind can focus on objectives, thankfulness, and the future God has for us. However, doubt likes to take up all the room too. We know doubt is in there when we are having thoughts like worry, upset feelings, or we are trying to figure out solutions to problems on our own. Faith and doubt can *never* occupy the same space and produce results that come from the Lord (James 1:6).

When our mind becomes preoccupied with our trouble, we are unable to focus our complete attention on anything else. That happens because, just like in the airplane bathroom, faith is waiting outside the door of our minds, while doubt finishes up.

If our mind has an "occupied with doubt" light on, it means we are too concerned with the problem we're facing to be open for any thoughts of faith in God's promises. Even in times of trouble, our lives will always have things going on. Our mind should still be able to process all those things *and* focus attention on everything else we need to be doing. We will only be able to successfully focus our attention on other things when we turn our mind's "occupied with faith" light on.

Picture our mind's thoughts like a highway. When trouble, doubt, and worry show up it's like an accident on the highway of our mind. Once an accident occurs, all the emergency crews have to arrive and clear the problem. Instead of positive flowing thoughts on our highway, our minds gets backed up while the clean-up crew works to clear the scene of worry, doubt, and trouble. Meanwhile, every other thought in our head, including peace, gets backed up for miles behind it unable to get where it needs to go.

Other thoughts we have will begin to get angry or impatient when they are unable to get where they want to go fast enough, much like we behave when we sit in traffic. When we sit in traffic we use our mouths to complain about it. However, sitting in traffic isn't usually as big a deal as we make it out to be. When our mind is in traffic, it will complain openly as well. Our mind will cause us to worry about things we don't usually get upset over, and the things that aren't really a big deal.

When our problems get piled up we might say, "I just can't deal with that right now too," "I'm under enough pressure," or "I can't believe I have to deal with all of that, on top of what I'm already dealing with!" Those types of expressions surface because the normal thoughts we are generally able to handle become harder to focus on when we are preoccupied. Little problems begin to feel like a pile up of big problems, but it is actually the problem of our lack of peace that is causing our frustrations to pour out into every area.

This congestion in our minds is caused by preoccupied thoughts. Accidents happen, and trouble will find us all, but being efficient at clearing the path, and getting everything unblocked, will allow our focus to be present for all of our life, and not just the worst parts of it.

Finding our faith in God quickly and putting it into action by praying for peace is one way to remove worry. However, the world often expects and encourages us to vent our frustrations by sharing them with everyone. We feel better when we let everyone know how tough we have it. However, that brief feeling of relief we get when we vent isn't peace. When we vent we are feeding our sin nature, and pleasing ourselves, by letting others believe we have problems even God can't handle.

We can't declare our problems to the world when trouble comes because believers *know* that Christ will help us overcome them (John 16:33). If we have faith Christ will remove our problems, it's like not having any problems at all. Believers understand that declaring our problems out loud will turn a one problem accident into a thirty problem pileup.

> *"Peace I leave with you; my peace I give to you. Not as the world gives do I give to you. Let not your hearts be troubled, neither let them be afraid."* **John 14:27 (ESV)**

Our peace comes from sharing our problems with God and not from sharing our problems with the world through our negative words and behavior. When we act negatively, we are building our doubt to believe there is not a solution to our problems. Our faith should realize that Jesus overcame so that there will always be a way for us to overcome as well.

Preoccupation is very easy to diagnose. If we are preoccupied with our problems, it means we haven't actually given them to God. We are preoccupied when our problems consume us, and they become all we can think about. When we are preoccupied, it means we are trying to self soothe, and not allowing our faith in God to let us overcome.

We see this in the movies a lot, when a character that goes through a bad break up and we see them on the couch in their sweats for weeks or months following. Later in the film, their friends usually have to come by, clean them up, and encourage them to move on by telling them that what happened is not the end of the world. This is relatable for many of us for how we deal with tough times.

We have a tendency to dwell on problems for so long as we try to figure out what happened and what's going to happen. We do it so much that the other areas of our lives begin to become unimportant to us. That is when we wind up on the couch looking dirty, smelling bad, and surrounded by pizza boxes. There is no peace at that pity party.

We need to be using our faith as payment to God to keep us from our own personal pity parties.

If our car broke down on the highway, most of us would call a tow truck to come pick it up and take it to the shop. At the shop, we would pay them to fix our car, so we could get back to what we were doing. We probably wouldn't sit in our car for a week when our car broke down wondering why it happened, figure out how we'll get to work next month, or wait for days for help. However, there are actually problems we face, where we exhibit that type of behavior.

Problems from break ups to layoffs are left on the side of the road simply because we don't have a "shop to take it to." God has clear solutions for our problems and we shouldn't be leaving them on the side of the road. It may take a lot of work to follow God's path of solution, but our problems can be fixed. We shouldn't sit there for months wondering why our life broke down, we should be searching out for help.

God is our tow truck and our mechanic. God will come and pick us up off the side of the road, take us to get our problems fixed, and get us back on the road to where we were going. God only has one form of currency He accepts as payment, and it isn't cash or checks or a credit card.

God fixes every problem imaginable and only accepts faith as payment for His service in our lives.

We are in peace when we are not spending every waking moment worried about the outcome of one situation in our lives that are full of situations. Our faith for God's will in our lives is activated through prayer and hearing the Word of God. Our faith will then act as payment to allow God to come clear up any accident in our lives. Doing other things without being preoccupied is how we *know* we have achieved peace and also how we know our faith is working.

Filling Time with Busy Work

We just learned that spending time focused on other things is a sign of peace. Filling our time with busy work is not the same thing and can sometimes be confused for actually having peace. This form of unrest isn't as easy to spot as the unrest in a preoccupied person might be.

Another key to determining if we are experiencing heavenly peace is recognizing busy work behavior as a coping mechanism for problems. We often use busy work to mask our hearts, and make others think we are doing better, but it may actually lower the number of opportunities for us to hear the encouragement we may need to search out and find peace from God.

There is no greater need for peace than the period of time after we experience death of a loved one. Busy work behavior and unrest is probably most easily visible around this time as well. The family of the deceased will often ask to help in any way they can. It's common to hear someone at funeral events say something like, "I just need to do something to take my mind off of things."

Wanting to be a help and not be overwhelmed by grief is a natural and understandable thing, but God wants us to take our mind off of our grief and place it on Him, so He can provide us with peace.

Testimony

I have a small family, and at an early age, experienced the death of my father. I speak candidly when I say that I blamed God for my dad's death because I didn't understand why a loving and caring God would take my dad from me. I sought no peace and spent many years after my father's death wondering what happened, instead of, drawing myself closer to God.

I retreated from God for many years and made it a point to keep myself a safe distance from Him. Instead of being welcomed into the arms of Jesus to feel the warmth of peace that only He can provide, I ran far away from Him.

I now know my father's death was not caused by God, and He is not to blame. The enemy comes to kill, steal, and destroy (John 10:10). The enemy killed my dad early, stole my time with God, and destroyed many years of my life following that event by leading my thoughts to disbelief in God and a lack of faith in God's love for me.

It is likely that the death of loved ones has kept many others from the Lord. I pray now that people know that God uses times of great loss to reveal himself to the hearts of those who are grieving. Those who have lost love ones can seek God and find the peace He distributes.

Filling our lives with busy work to take our minds off our problems isn't actually a solution to problems, but instead covers them up. Makeup works this same way. Makeup covers up blemishes and pimples and gives a look that everything is better than it is. Busy work, just like make up, keeps a person's true complexion, or faith, hidden from view, and makes the problems unnoticeable. Busy work is our makeup for peace.

Busy work hides us from being vulnerable, and without vulnerability, it is hard to experience faith in that area. Vulnerability is not a weakness, but an act of submission that allows us to reach out to God for help.

We need to watch ourselves and be able to recognize if we are exhibiting busy work behavior the next time we face a problem. We should also look to see if others are struggling by presenting busy work symptoms. Watch for signs like avoiding the subject, wanting to do more than usual, wanting to go out more than usual, electing to volunteer themselves for too much, and for comments that tell everyone "how busy they are."

If we notice one of these things in our lives, or the lives of others, they can be signs of distraction and unrest. We should reach out to that person if we can. We could take a moment to sit down with them to talk, and let them know it is okay to not have it all figured out right away. Remind them that God does have it all figured out and offer to pray with them in order to ask God for peace over this situation.

If this is a familiar situation in our own lives, we should take a moment to understand we aren't actually fixing anything by covering up our problems with busy work. Wanting to feign peace to impress others by pretending we're okay isn't actually going to help us feel better. That behavior defers peace, and if we are dealing with something, we need to get peace on our hearts quickly to stop the hurting.

Our faith gets stalled while we are distracting ourselves. It is God's desire for us to concentrate on Him and not ignore the problem, but rather lay it at His feet. Busy work is our makeup that conceals how little peace we really have. When we are without peace, we are without faith. When we are without faith, we are stuck where we are, and we have no vision for God's future for our lives. Our joy is directly connected to our future. Finding faith leads to peace and joy.

Trouble Sleeping

Sleep behavior is another key to determining if we have achieved peace. This method of observation is great for two reasons. First, sleep is simple to observe because we can't fake it. Second, having sweet sleep provides us with a clear ability to realize if we have found faith in God.

> *"If you lie down, you will not be afraid; when you lie down, your sleep will be sweet."* **Proverbs 3:24 (NIV)**

Sleep is an essential part of a healthy life. A good night's sleep of seven to eight hours allows our bodies and minds a chance to rest, recharge, and heal. This is the way God intended our bodies to work. The enemy knows the importance of sleep and understands if we are without peaceful sleep, we are dragging, our minds aren't sharp, and we are weakened against future attacks. God promises us sweet sleep in Proverbs 3:24, so that we know the enemy cannot steal our sleep away from us.

When we lay down to sleep it is quiet, the rest of the world is leaving us alone, and we are just left with our thoughts. Our thoughts are the battlefield, and we are at war with ourselves. Thankfully, we know from Ephesians 6 that God gave us all kinds of armor to protect ourselves.

While we are trying to sleep, our mind is either at rest, which allows for a good night's sleep, or our mind races back and forth thinking about the trouble tomorrow brings us, which leads us have troubled sleep.

When we don't lay our problems at God's feet or don't cast all anxiety and worry to Him, then we have to keep and carry all those problems with us. That's a sobering thought; isn't it?

Do you think we can feel peace if the weight of all those problems are on our shoulders?

That is why sleep is so important, and sweet sleep is only available when we give our troubles to God. That means if we don't give them up we will be forced to listen to that battle being fought in our mind on how to handle the situation.

How can we have peace when there are still problems in our future to face?

When we have peace from God, it doesn't mean we forgot all about the problems; instead, having peace means our worries have left us. It is a sign of peace in our lives when the pit in our stomach is not there, and we are able to focus our thoughts on things other than our problems.

There is a solution if we are trying to sleep and, instead, find ourselves tossing and turning, unable to get comfortable because of the panic, doubt, or worry running through our minds. We aren't talking about the solution of using medicine to put us to sleep, but rather, the remedy of prayer.

Faith in God isn't active without prayer. If we aren't in prayer, then we aren't giving our problems to God, and allowing Him to take good care of them. Without prayer, our worry will increase, and spread to other areas of our life, including our sleep, and we will find it is a constant struggle to find relaxation. If we aren't spending time in prayer, we will rack our brains trying to come up with solutions to our problems on our own. We need to remember that the solution we come up with will never be as satisfying as the one God wants us to use.

Do you remember a time when your parents took care of you when you were sick as a kid?

As children when we are overcome with sickness, we had no idea how to fight it on our own. We rely entirely on our parents for help. It is natural for us to rely on someone for help as a child. It is also natural for the parents of a sick child to want them to get better and to take care of them. These responses are inside of us because we were made in God's image and that is how God does things. God is our Heavenly Father, and He desires for us to get better, and He will do whatever it takes to help us.

Using our faith was natural to us as a sick child. We used faith that our parents would pick out the right medicine, take us to the doctor if needed, and get us things we wanted that would comfort us like ice cream, clear soda, or special toys. We relied on our parents to check our temperature and tell us what we needed to do to get better, and how it would work. God as our heavenly parent is no different.

When we are sick or troubled and we ask for God's help, He provides just like our parents did. When we are little, we just assume our parents will do all of those things for us. We were never surprised when they would do something for us because we expected them to be there for us. Our faith in God should work no differently.

Trouble sleeping is a giant we sometimes need to fight against. We can't let sleep become another thing the enemy tries to take from us. Sweet sleep belongs to us and is a promise of God. When we release all our thoughts to God in prayer, we allow ourselves to overcome that battle in our minds. When we pray, all we need to do is just start talking to Him. We can say something like, "God, I'm not sure how I'm going to get through this," or "I really need your help."

No solution we can come up with to solve our problems will work the way we want it to. Unforeseen events, distractions, and more problems will detour us from the best solution. God sees all of those things, and accounts for them. Since we can't make adjustments for our unknown future, we need God to come and take care of our problems for us.

After a faithful prayer, our mind will begin to be still. God is our provider and will grant us our hearts desires. Praying for sleep isn't what we think of, when we think of what an important prayer sounds like. However, sweet sleep is a vital part of our life, health, and recovery. Without prayers protecting our sweet sleep, it will be vulnerable to attacks.

We are now equipped with the knowledge that sleep is meant to be good and peaceful and allow our bodies and minds to stay healthy. Use that information to receive the promise of God. When we find sweet sleep, we will *know* that we have peace and also know that we have found faith.

Complaining and Questioning

A key to determining if we have achieved peace from God is by recognizing the speech we are using. Our words are determined by our thinking, which in turn, determines our behavior. Our faith for God's will to be done in our life can be deterred in many ways, and not one of them is more destructive than our own words. The Bible says there is life and death in the power of the tongue (Prov. 18:21).

When we feel discouraged or are lacking peace, it is easy to reach for negative words, comments, and questions to make us feel better or to lash out at those we think caused our problems. Negative words are common place in our lives, and we are all susceptible to using them.

Why do we commonly use negative words to describe our problems? Why are we more likely to complain and question our situations than we are to talk faithfully about their solutions?

The answer is in our language.

A study was done in 2005 at Penn State on language development. This secular study brought to light an extraordinary result.

A study done on the English language provided the following statistics:

- 60% of the words in our language are negative or have negative connotations.
- 20% of the words in our language are positive or have positive connotations.
- 20% of the words in our language are neutral.

The study determined our negative words were in abundance because we think we need extra words to accurately describe our tough situations. We did that so we would not confuse the listener into thinking our situation is easy to handle.

If we are having a positive day, we might use words like good, awesome, or great to describe how happy we are. When we are happy, we think that those few words are enough to accurately describe our positive moments.

On the other hand, if we are having a tough time, we don't think words like sad or bad are enough words to accurately describe the moment we are facing. To fix the problem of needing more words to describe our trouble, we came up with more accurate ones. We now use words like depressing, terrible, gross, sickening, awful, unbelievable, distraught, broken, messed up, and a multitude of curse words to share our problems with others.

While we may not realize how much power our words have behind them, our enemy surely does. We know this because we can tell through this study that our language is under attack. The enemy has been behind the scenes adding new ways to declare doubt out of our mouths. It was done in such a way that we didn't even notice.

The negative additions to our language by the enemy make it much easier to compose a sentence with negative words than it is with positive ones. The enemy wants us to use negative words because he knows our faith in God doesn't work when those words are spoken.

Think about how hard it is to use words to be positive, when 6 out of every 10 words in our language disable faith in God.

We are at a severe disadvantage with our words, and we didn't even know it. No wonder it is so easy for us to talk negatively. We don't know many other words. Thankfully, we now have the knowledge of the importance of our words because we see what heavy attack our language is under. The enemy attacks hardest what God finds important, and he seems to have launched a large scale attack against our words. We need to equip ourselves with understanding and wisdom to correct our thinking and change our behavior towards how we speak.

We see that our language is filled with negative words. We know that we can't find a solution without opening our mouths. We also know that we will find trouble every day, and that trouble will need to be described by our words in prayer.

So, how do we know when we are using the right words?

We know we are using words of faith if the words that come out of our mouths are not complaints and questioning comments.

"Why is this happening to me," or "I can't believe I have to go through this," are some examples of how we are unknowingly disabling our faith. These words are usually the first thoughts that go through our heads when trouble comes, and in turn, those are the first types of words that come out of our mouths when we talk about our problems to others.

In order to prevent negative words from being staples of our "perceived problem solving" diet, we need to get them out of our heads. We are not finding peace from God in our hearts, if these words are coming out of our mouths.

To change our words, we need to change the way we initially think about problems when they show up. This is not an easy thing to do; it will take lots of practice and mega grace from God for us to become able to take these steps when trouble comes. We find faith by staying positive and *knowing* that God has a solution to our troubles. We need to declare God's promises and try to remember to leave negative talk unsaid, and it will leave our faith open to seeing positive results.

Part Eight:
Finding Faith for Today

Today's Keys of Faith

"So don't worry about tomorrow, for tomorrow will bring its own worries. Today's trouble is enough for today."
Matthew 6:34 (NLT)

If you only take one thing from this book, and use it to strengthen your faith for God's will to be done in your life, it should be that verse.

Our faith in God starts and ends with how we see our future. If we are worried about tomorrow, we don't see a good future for our lives because we can't see past our circumstances; therefore, we cannot have faith in God's will being done in our lives. If we are not worried about tomorrow, it's because our faith in God *knows* that His future for our lives is bright, regardless of our circumstances. The greatest worry we will ever face is our unknown future. Worry is the worst enemy of faith. If we are worried, we are in doubt. Doubt disables faith.

When we are in worry mode we often ask ourselves these types of questions:

How will I afford it? When will I get better? What do I do now? Who is going to help me? Why am I not doing better?

These are just a few common, every day questions asked by people all over the world that are only asked because we lack faith, yet they are inevitable because when we have these questions in our heads, we begin to get burdened by wanting their answers. We need to let go of these questions and remember when we give our problems to God, our burden will be light (Matt. 11:30).

Finding faith for God today is rooted in how we see our future. If we look forward with hope to the future that God will provide for us, our faith for today's problems are secure (Prov. 4:25). God wants us to know that our faith protects us today, and that tomorrow is not more important. If we can live with faith that God will take care of our needs to be protected, watched over, and taken care of every day, then, tomorrow's problems will never worry us.

The enemy knows that when we have faith for God today, we will be protected tomorrow. That is why the devil wants us to look at our future with great concern. If we are concerned about our future, we won't live in faith today. If we worry about tomorrow, we won't put up our shields of faith today, and we won't protect ourselves from fiery darts.

Trying not to worry when we are under attack is not easy. The moment we decide to walk in the path of promises designed for us by God, we will be confronted with that sin nature. Our sin nature is designed to talk us out of God's promises.

Adam and Eve were confronted by sin in the Garden of Eden. They ate the forbidden fruit and lost their promises from God. Losing promises, is the same thing that happens to us when God shows us a better future, and the devil talks us out of it by making us doubt that a good future is possible or even worth wanting.

To separate ourselves from our sin nature and follow the path God laid out for our lives, we will need to rely on the faith we have today. Having faith in God for tomorrow's blessings is unnecessary if we are unable to battle the enemy today. Matthew 6:34 is our reminder to not let ourselves get defeated today because tomorrow won't matter if we do.

To find faith for God's promises today, we need to let anything that troubles us about tomorrow go. That behavior comes from the understanding that lots of things can happen between today and tomorrow. The only thing we can actually change about tomorrow is how we think about it. We can't stop tomorrow from happening or hold off its problems, but if we are focused on all the bad stuff that might happen tomorrow, then we won't focus on all the good stuff God is doing for us *today*.

To build our faith, we need to focus our attention on today's moments and bringing God into them. The eventual hope is that we will train ourselves to have the faith in God that allows us to not be worried about the future at all because we are so confident in God to take care of today's troubles.

The keys listed below will help us find faith in God for today. These keys contain many insights, strategies, and wisdom we can use to train our faith. We can also use this list as a reference to check back to on hard days or when we see dark clouds in our days ahead. Either way, when we begin to implement these lessons we learn from these keys into our lives today, we will be blessed with faith in God that doesn't worry about tomorrow.

Keys to Find Faith for Today

- **Dwell on Tasks We Can Accomplish TODAY**
- **Be Thankful for Blessings We Have TODAY**
- **Sing Songs of Praise and Scripture TODAY**
- **Believe in God for a Blessing TODAY**
- **Find Scripture to Declare TODAY**
- **Share Our Heart TODAY**

Dwell on Tasks We Can Accomplish TODAY

While it's true we shouldn't worry about tomorrow's problems, it doesn't mean we can't work on them today. So, how do we work on tomorrow's problems without worrying about them?

First, we need to know what our problem is. Knowing our *exact* problem allows our prayers to be focused on what we need help with. For example, if our tax bill is due, it's better to know and pray for God to provide us with the resources to pay the exact total bill of $487.38, than it is to know we have a tax bill in our pile of other bills and just pray for God to get us out of debt.

217

God keeps excellent records. God likes things to have order. God knows the hairs on our head, and our days are numbered (Luke 12:7; Ps. 139:16). Those numbers change every day. God keeps good records, and He expects us to as well. When God gave plans to Noah to build an ark, He didn't say "Noah, you should build me an ark." Instead, God told Noah the exact measurements of the boat. Noah was then able to believe for exactly what He needed to complete God's will.

We are often filled with worry, entirely because we don't actually assess the situation. We make wide assumptions like, "My car won't make that trip," or "There is no way I can live on that." When in reality, we are not focused on the exact problem. The key to accomplishing things for tomorrow is to write down the exact problem and pray for its solution, today.

Our prayer may look like this:

"God, I am thankful you have a plan for me to overcome this. I ask for peace over my worry and ask for strength to lay this problem at your feet. Please give me the wisdom to put in motion the steps I need to take to claim victory over this. Amen."

Don't forget that God works outside the box to give solutions to prayer. If this is our first prayer over a particular problem, then we should realize that all of the solutions we had in our mind before that first prayer were likely not from God; those were our own thoughts. That was us trying to figure out a solution to our own situation and not us giving it to God.

After we pray, God may give us new thoughts. God may tell us how to handle our situation by giving us a thought in our head that wasn't there before or by giving us an idea or task that sounds like something we may not want to do. We should be listening for and believing God will direct our steps (Prov. 16:9; Jer. 29:11).

Why does God give us answers to prayer this way? God likes to stretch our faith by sending us down the road less travelled. Taking a road we may not want to go down to solve a problem is God's way of polishing our sharp edges and preparing our faith in God for future events.

When we dwell on things we can accomplish today, like going to work, getting food or clothes, and supplies for today's needs, we are filling our mind with objectives. Objectives overthrow the space doubt takes up in our head, and keeps our worries about tomorrow out as well. When we are motivated to accomplish God's checklist for our lives, we are focusing on His promises for our future, and not the problems of tomorrow.

Be Thankful for Blessings We Have TODAY

When facing a problem, our first thoughts are usually trouble. Troubling thoughts, will naturally lead us to worry, unless of course, we are trained to find faith first. When our mind is racing, we are unable to reflect on what good things we have to be thankful about which is a key to our door of finding faith for today.

This key to finding faith in God relies on our ability to be thankful, even in times of trouble, for all that we have. Trouble finds us all, and sometimes that trouble removes people, relationships, and possessions from our lives. The key to being faithful today is recognizing that God has a plan to redeem us from what we've lost, and our thankfulness for the things we have today is the faithful behavior we can exhibit to see that plan succeed.

When tough times come, we need to let our first thoughts be of thankfulness. God's Word says to be thankful in all things and that includes trouble (1 Thess. 5:18). Whatever we are facing, there are still blessings in our lives. We can be thankful we had food to eat, a roof to sleep underneath, or someone who loves us in our lives. Those are all blessings, even if one of them is the problem area, the other ones may not be. When we thank God for our blessings, it brings Him great joy, and also lets God know that we appreciate all that He does for our lives.

God responds to praise. It is no different than when someone is really thankful to us for something we did for them. We all feel warm inside when we receive thanks. After being thanked by someone, we are much more excited at the possibility of giving to them again because we know they appreciate it.

We need to recognize some of our current blessings, and spend time *today* thanking God for them.

Did you get food in your stomach today? Did you put gasoline in your vehicle today? Did you buy groceries today? Did you have heat/air conditioning in your home today? Is there anything you can be thankful for today? Tell Him!

God is so generous, but He also likes to know He is appreciated. Our first thought is not usually to be thankful during a high stress situation or while facing big problems, but we already said that focusing on faith for today was *not* going to be easy. During our day, we can help ease the trouble on our hearts by spending some time taking an inventory of good things from *today*.

If we need to find faith for today, all we need to do is be thankful. We already said it's hard to be thankful when everything around us seems to be falling apart. That's why really being thankful is an act of faith. Sometimes our circumstances don't give us a reason to be thankful. We are supposed to be thankful anyway. It is vital to our success as believers to be thankful every day for something God's will is providing to our lives.

Sing Songs of Praise and Scripture TODAY

"This is the day the LORD has made. We will rejoice and be glad in it." **Psalm 118:24 (NLT)**

Psalm 118:24 is not just a scripture, but it is also a song. Singing is a great way to remember and declare verses of scripture. God moves on His Word, so we should constantly be declaring the promises of scripture and asking God to deliver those promises for us.

Singing songs is also a great tool for memorization. I'm sure many of us still remember the words to songs we listened to when we were younger. They are implanted deep inside our mind. Imagine if the songs of praise and scripture were implanted deep in our mind to recall whenever we needed it. God could flow into our life easily and without much thought or effort.

An easy key to finding faith for today is our ability to sing songs that apply God's Word to *today's* situation. Declaring God's promises through scripture get God moving to clear the troubled path from our lives. Singing when distressed is difficult, much like laughing is when we are angry, but overcoming our troubles through singing songs that glorify Him is a sign that we have found faith in God today.

The great Biblical example of someone finding faith for today by singing is found when Paul, while locked in prison, sang hymns to God (Acts 16:25). Paul was in the worst place he could be, in a situation none of us would want for ourselves. Instead of complaining or worrying, Paul lifted up praises of scripture to the Lord because he knew God would provide a better future for him.

Many of today's most popular Christian artists use scripture to fill their verses and choruses. So, even if we don't know a scripture that applies directly to the problems we are facing, we could sing a song we know and bring God's Word in our lives. Worshipping God by singing any song of praise will lead to faith for today because it is difficult to sing to the Lord without a heart that believes the Lord does wonderful things for His people (Ps. 96:3).

Believe in God for a Blessing TODAY

A key to building our faith in God is to exercise it often. Believing in God to provide our lives with something today is a simple method we can use to exercise our faith. When our faith is in use, it blocks all the doubts we have for tomorrow from taking root in our minds. Believing God will provide our lives with victories today will keep our faith occupied.

When Jesus withered the fig tree, He told Peter that event occurred because of faith (Mark 11:21-22). Jesus used His faith for God's will to be done in His life every day. Jesus asked God to help Him feed, serve, and heal others. Jesus said our faith is responsible for the results of our actions (Mark 9:23). One reason Jesus lived without worry was because He demonstrated the faith to see God's will done in His life every day (John 5:19).

Every day, we should pray our expectations to Christ. We can pray to see Him bless our lives, heal our friends, or see a family member find salvation. Every day is an opportunity to see God move in our lives and another way we can find faith for today.

Did you wake up this morning believing you wouldn't eat all day or that you wouldn't get to see your family? Were the first thoughts in your mind when you woke up was that your work wouldn't want you to come in or that your car wasn't going to start today?

No! Instead, you woke up *expecting* all of those things to happen. You expected you would eat, see your family, and go to work. Expecting life to work out is what faith is.

God wants us to tackle every problem with that type expectation or hope. Another key to find faith for today is to wake up with complete *expectation* that the life God has planned for us is going to work out for our good (Rom. 8:28). It may be tough, and we'll face problems we have to conquer, but God has a plan to pull us through all of those things.

I don't believe many of us actually realize how much faith we exert on a daily basis by believing things will just work out. Our expectations have been the reason God has been supplying all we need in our daily lives. If we realized how much God was providing for our faith, we would spend more time thanking Him for all the things He does and spend less time worried about if He is going to quit supplying our needs.

Find Scripture to Declare TODAY

When our day is turned towards worry or doubt sometimes the fastest way to gain peace over that situation is scripture. Praying scripture provides relief that we just can't get anywhere else.

God watches over His Word, and He cannot lie. If the Bible contains a promise to us in it, and we declare that promise over our situation, God *has to move* (Jer. 1:12). Otherwise, God would be a liar, and everything we believe is wrong. However, God is not a liar, and He has an action plan for our life that puts us into a place where that plan can get executed when we ask Him to move on His Word.

A key to finding faith for today is to learn what God promises us through scripture and understand that when we pray those scriptures over our lives and have faith in them today, we will see them fulfilled in our lives. There is nothing more powerful we can say to defeat our troubles than the Words of God (Heb. 4:12).

Praying scripture is our real life way of getting promises fulfilled, but we need to know the exact promises of God, so we know how we can expect to be blessed.

We all like to pray for blessings, but if we don't know the promises God wants to bless us with in the Bible, how can we really pray and believe those promises to come?

Let's pretend God has a promise to hand deliver us a blessing to our mailbox on Wednesday. Let's say we pray for that blessing, and then go and camp out by the mailbox on Saturday. As time passes, and it doesn't come we will begin to doubt Him. God's promise *is* on its way, but we are waiting four days earlier than it is set to arrive.

What if Tuesday comes, and we decide we are tired of waiting and allow doubt to move us away from the mailbox, and we miss out on the blessing completely. We were one day from receiving our blessing, but we didn't because we didn't know the exact promise of God was to deliver our promise on Wednesday.

We cannot expect to be blessed if we don't know how God plans on blessing us. The Bible contains all the answers, but we need to get those verses in our hearts so that our faith in Christ can allow us to receive those promises.

Doubt uses time and our lack of knowledge as its entry points to attack our faith. Speaking the scripture over our situation and knowing the promise God affords for that situation is crucial. We need to declare the truth in prayer over our lives, and God's Word is the truth!

When we equip ourselves with the knowledge of specific verses, our faith for today will increase. When we know what promises of

God to expect, and we recognize the arrival of those promises, our faith will be overflown, and our expectations will become increased. The bigger our faith in God the more we will be able to receive His will in our lives.

When we receive blessings, God can use them to show off His love to those around us. Our blessings from God will make those that do not have Jesus envious, and they will desire a relationship with Him for themselves (Rom. 11:11).

Share Our Heart TODAY

Have you ever found yourself facing a tough day, an uphill battle, or a moment that seems insurmountable? On those days wouldn't you rather go back to bed, and pretend like it never happened?

This "solution" while many would say sounds like a perfect one is just not the way to deal with problems.

Another key to finding faith for God today is to lay our doubts and worries at the feet of Jesus. We aren't always able to do that, even though God wants us to. Finding faith in God will always be a struggle, and that's why there are many different ways to find, and use, it in our lives. However, when we recognize the power of unloading our burdens, we will be free to walk in God's will instead of hiding under the covers.

We already thanked Him, made lists, prayed, and quoted scripture. Is there really anything left we can do? Yes. Tough days and moments are meant to be shared. No moment is meant to be quieted.

When we do something successful, don't we want to tell someone about it? Do we sometimes get mad if we call someone, and they don't answer the phone so we can tell them *right now*? Kids like to show off all the time, "Look what I did," or "Watch this." We like to share our triumphs *and* our disappointments with others.

We feel better when we accomplish something and then share it with someone. It also feels better when we are struggling to share them with someone.

Have you ever heard someone really share his or her struggles? Have you ever seen someone do that, and then say something like, "That's a load off," "I'm so glad to get that off my chest," or I feel so much better now that I talked about it?"

We feel better after we talk to others because God designed us to share (1 Thess. 2:8). We share with God in prayer, share our time with others, and share our lives with our family. This was God's design, and when we are going against the grain of God by keeping everything to ourselves. Our lives will always feel so much better when we finally let go of our problems and start moving in the direction of God, by voicing and confessing our burdens to Him.

Our peace in a situation is often at its highest after a good conversation. It doesn't matter whether that conversation is in prayer, with a family member, or a friend. We weren't meant to keep thoughts locked inside us. Holding in our thoughts is like being underwater for a long time, and then coming up for air, we just gasp for it once we get it, but the feeling is incredible. That need to share is also why we are sometimes physically able to see a drastic difference in a person before and after a conversation in which they unload burdens.

Conversations bring perspective. The Bible tells us that it is good to have a *multitude* of wise counselors (Prov. 24:6). Many counselors bring different ideas, allow us to see all the angles, and ultimately, provide victory. Even though not every angle will look right to us, and not every opinion should be listened to. God uses others to speak His Word into us. God uses these tough life moments to uplift and encourage each other through.

God doesn't want us to face any moment alone. Finding Faith for *today* in moments can sometimes be very difficult. Why does our faith increase *today* when we open our mouths and confess our problems or struggles to God, friends, or family?

Our faith increases because talking gets our problem out in the open. We said earlier that it is good to write down *exactly* what the problem is we need to pray for. Opening our mouths about our problems is just like writing it down because it gets the *exact* problem out on the table, and allows us to be encouraged that it will turn out alright through specific prayer to God.

Talking with others is just another avenue God uses to remove doubts from our mind. A good person in our life will never tell us things like, "Well, you're not going to make it through this," "Don't tell me this I was having a good day," "I don't want to hear about your problems," "You *should* be depressed," or "I don't know why you keep trying." If they do, we should not surround ourselves with them.

Good people to have in our lives are ones who will encourage us. We need to surround our lives with people that will help frame our thoughts to realize our situation can always get better. God does this same thing when we pray.

Our faith gets restored, and our doubts get pushed aside, when we realize God will create a path for our future to get better than what today looks like right now. Our joy is directly related to our level of faith in God. The greater faith we have today, the greater joy we will have today too. In order to have joy *today*, we need to build our faith, by sharing our lives with others.

The Bible says more about the topic of friendship than the topics of Heaven and Hell combined. God desires us to have good friends because God knows that good friends are an essential part of a productive life. Without good friends, our struggles will be that much harder to overcome.

Bad friends can't help our problems the right way, and they usually bring more problems and stress with them, than they bring solutions. Sharing problems with good friends is an opportunity to remove doubt and worry and replace it with thoughts of God's brighter future.

Finding faith in God is directly connected with how we see the future His will has for our lives. Good friends will remind us it's going to get better. Faith comes by hearing and hearing that our life will get better is a great way to remove ourselves from a "hide in bed" situation. Faith for *today* is so important because the faster you let go and let God the faster God can help *today*.

My Testimony of Finding Faith for Today

A few months after God called me into ministry He asked me to quit my full-time job. I was very skeptical. My family was not entirely supportive. I wasn't sure I would even do it. Then I started to read stories of people who had big faith like Peter, James, and John who all left their jobs to go into ministry.

God showed me all the names of *big* faith listed in Hebrews 11. I began to see that people who are able to take those big leaps when God calls are the ones He always gets to show off through. My spirit got excited to be a vessel for God; however, my brain was not excited.

My first thought was doubt and worry about not having enough money. Why would God not want me to have an immediate source of income? If I have been called for His purpose, wouldn't He want me to have money to live? Many around me thought quitting my job was stupid and reckless. Quitting a paying job to start a ministry was not seen as a logical step of faith by most people.

I began to ask God for confirmation before I stepped out in faith in such a big way. I knew this couldn't be a situation I relied only on my own discernment of the Holy Spirit. I needed more than that, and I knew if God wanted me to quit my choice for a job and take the job that followed Jesus, He would hear my prayers and, hopefully, do more to build my faith.

I had read the stories that said Abraham and Sarah were sent angels, and Moses was sent a burning bush when God wanted them to do something. I figured it wasn't outside the line of faith to pray that I could have confirmation like that too. I didn't need a burning bush, but I knew God could do something to confirm His calling on my life. So I prayed for God to speak to me in a way that was impossible to ignore and that I would receive confirmation from multiple sources that this is what He was calling me to do.

One day while driving into work, I was listening to a local Christian radio station that played fifteen minute sections of sermons all day long. This pastor came on the radio and gave a message about taking big leaps of faith and following what God asks you to do even though no one around you seems to hear the same thing. I felt like this message was pointed at me. In fact, during the message itself the pastor said word for word this sentence, "If God calls you to leave your job, then you should leave your job." I couldn't believe it. Was God talking to me? Surely, that was a coincidence. So again, I prayed for God to show me more and confirm that God wanted me to follow Him in ministry.

Then, as I continued to drive, I found myself driving behind a semi-truck. Normally, I would fly around it, but for whatever reason I was so zoned in with the message I was hearing that I didn't worry about speeding to work. I wasn't really concerned or noticing that my trip was being slowed down by this semi-truck. When I finally looked up and realized that I had been behind it for quite a while I decided to pass it. At that point I saw something on the back of the truck. As I looked closer, I thought, "That can't be what I think it is! Can it?" It was a sticker. The sticker had the word "Faith" written above the Bible verse, Philippians 4:13. This was a commercial truck. What commercial truck have you ever seen with Bible verse decals on it? I was again taken aback. I took a picture because it was so unusual. I thought again, "Was God talking to me? That's just a sticker; that's not God." I prayed again, "God, I need more".

As I pulled into work I got a phone call from my close Christian friend, Kevin. Kevin knew of my call and knew that I was waiting to make a decision, but He didn't know I had been praying for confirmation. After I said hello, he said "I just heard from the Lord. He has told me to tell you to quit your job, and not to worry because you can stay with me, and we will figure it out. I don't want you to worry about the rent. I'll take care of it." I started to get overwhelmed; I said that I had just gotten a couple messages and was starting to feel like God was really pushing me.

My mind raced. I thought, "Is this real? Why does God want me? Is this really what I'm supposed to do with my life?"

I went into work, and these thoughts preoccupied my mind all day. Eventually, I decided that none of what had happened that day was enough to convince me that God wanted me to leave my job. I thought those things, while encouraging, weren't enough for me to quit the safety and security I felt my job provided. While working, I prayed in my head and asked God, "If you want me to quit my job to come and work for you in ministry, can you tell me so loud that I can't miss it?" No sooner than I finish that prayer in my head, a customer sitting directly across from me, who hadn't said a word to me that day, said the following words to me:

"John, when are you going to leave this job."

Whoa.

I didn't know this person outside of work, and he didn't know my situation or that I was contemplating a decision like that in my mind. I almost started to cry. I asked the man why he said that to me. He responded, "I'm not sure really; it just looked like you were thinking about something, and I thought that was it." I knew then after all those prayers I knew *this moment* was God giving me my confirmation. It was my very own burning bush moment. No one will *ever* be able to dissuade my faith that wasn't a moment sent from God. I can't explain or understand it, but that's what happened. All I need to believe is that God was behind it, and that was evidence of God telling me to trust Him.

My mind raced again. How would this work? I'm not smart enough. I'm not Christian enough. How will I pay bills? How will I survive? Who on Earth is going to believe I've been called and want to listen to what God puts on my heart to say? Even though I had those thoughts, I tried not to dwell in them. Instead, I repeated the verse that was on the back of that truck.

> *"For I can do everything through Christ, who gives me strength."* **Philippians 4:13 (NLT)**

When I left my job, I cashed out a few thousand dollars from a 401(k). It was the only thing my gambling problem didn't destroy. I figured I would live off of that money, and by the time it ran out, God would have a new source of income for me.

A few months later that money had run its course. As I learned to steward my money, and my possessions, I realized at the beginning of the month that my budget would not allow me to fulfill the payment of the bills I owed at the end of the month. I would owe on my car payment and not have enough to cover it. It was a loan, and I knew if I missed a payment it was likely they would come and repossess it. When I went to the Lord in prayer, I asked for guidance. The only instructions I heard from Him was for me to tell no one about my struggles, and He would provide for me.

Not telling anyone about my struggles is especially hard for me. My whole life, mostly when I was gambling and constantly having money hardships, I reached out often to friends, family, and acquaintances, and asked for help financially when I needed it. My normal reaction was to figure out how to get myself out of trouble by asking someone for money. When God asked me specifically not to ask anyone for help but to put my trust solely in Him, it was very tough for me.

21 days. That's how long it was from the time I knew I didn't have enough to the time that I owed the money I didn't have. I woke up praying and asking the Lord to help me for 21 days. It became increasingly difficult as the days went by, and God hadn't yet supplied my need. I began to wonder why it hadn't come or if I was praying incorrectly.

I had support from many people in my life who would have given me the money to pay this bill if I asked. I knew it was important to for me to trust God in this situation, and I was trying to act in faith even though it was extremely difficult. God had called me into this position, so He must have a plan, but I couldn't see it in the natural.

A couple days before the bill was due I started to get really anxious. I almost told everyone how hard it was to be patient. I came very close to asking for help. I was spending nights on the ground praying to God, wondering where God was and asking Him if there was something else I needed to do. I proactively thanked God every day for providing for me, even though my blessing hadn't shown up yet, I was trying to have faith it would.

Then, the morning of the 21st day came. The bill was due that day. God hadn't yet given me the resources to pay it. I knew they would come and take my car from me if I was unable to pay. I went to bed the night before unsure about what would happen, but thanked God with my mouth through prayer for providing for me. I hadn't told anyone like He asked, and because I didn't ask anyone, I didn't know how my problem would actually be solved.

I woke up that morning beside myself. My emotions were high because I thought if my faith wasn't right enough to let Him pay a bill, how could my faith allow God to use me to lead a ministry?

The morning of the 21st day I prayed honestly and told God I trusted Him, and since I didn't have the money to pay my bill, it must be His will for me to lose my car for some reason. I was filled with peace. It was the first time I had peace during those 21 days. I knew if it was in God's will for me to lose my car than I would just have to get by life without it. God must have a reason I don't need it, and I know that I don't need to understand the reasons of God to be in faith. As I prayed that prayer, I began to experience God. He spoke to me, and God told me to go and check the mailbox. I began to cry. I knew what was out there before I looked.

Inside the mailbox was a plain white envelope addressed to me sitting right on top. Inside the envelope was a money order for the exact amount of money I needed to pay my car note that day. I couldn't believe it. I started yelling and thanking the Lord. This was the biggest miracle I had ever experienced in my life up to that point. I was so excited!!

On the 21st day God answered my prayer because of my faith. God showed up right on time, and He did it in an unexpected way.

The money was from a person I had never been blessed by before. When I reached out in order to thank them I was told the following story. They had heard I had started a ministry and wanted to bless me. They were planning on selling some furniture on Craigslist and were going to donate half of what they received to a couple different places. They said they wanted to send it sooner and had a smaller check written out, but the weirdest thing happened. They had promised the furniture to someone who never came to get it. A couple days later someone offered them *more* than what they were originally going to get for the furniture. They told me that because of that blessing to them, they would be generous and sew a bigger seed to me. In fact, they felt such a burden to get that new seed to me that they just sent the money out of their own account before they even cashed the check from the furniture.

God is always doing more behind the scenes to answer prayers then we will ever see, and I realized how much that was true when I was told their version of the story. God went through lots of steps to answer this "tiny" prayer. Since God went through all this to answer my "tiny" prayer, you can imagine all He would do to answer every single one of my "big" prayers as well.

After that, my entire life was in the hands of the Lord. It was a new level of faith for me. I had to begin to believe in God to provide every single thing I needed. It is very different than what many of us are used to. We can be thankful for what we have, but not many of us have to wake up praying for God to provide breakfast, lunch, dinner, and things like soap or other basics. We are simply just used to having them. After that moment, I began to realize how much I didn't depend on the Lord for many things. I never really knew all the comforts and needs I was used to having could be so difficult to come by. It really humbled me.

God is so good though. For months and months I had the luxury of waking up and asking God for little things, necessities, and also the bigger more long-term prayers. I got the opportunity to put my entire faith in the Lord in order to receive what I needed. God showed up, and still shows up, for me *every day*! I never missed a meal, I always had gas in my car, and my bills were always paid. God provided those things in ways I didn't expect or that I was used to. Many people have offered their help to me, and I have found many unexpected opportunities and countless blessings. The time after I left my job was crucial for me to understand exactly how much faith in God I didn't have and wasn't using. It taught me how much I needed to find faith for God's will to be done in my life today!

I'm telling you my story because trusting God is *so* important. Taking big leaps of faith when He calls you can change your life! All those worries I had about tomorrow, and all the doubt in my mind to stay where I was, could've easily prevented, and almost did, what God wanted from me. It was only through faith that I was able to give those worries to God and step "irrationally" out of the boat. Without faith, I wouldn't be writing this book, and more importantly, God wouldn't have been able to use me to share the gospel message with all the people this ministry has allowed me to meet.

Are your doubts and worries keeping you from accomplishing God's will?

Ask Him to confirm His role for you in His kingdom and faithfully follow that path once you hear from Him. Find your moment to walk on water towards Jesus!

Part Nine:
Finding Faith Fulfilled

Results of Finding Faith

> *"So the promise is received by faith. It is given as a free gift. And we are all certain to receive it, whether or not we live according to the law of Moses, if we have faith like Abraham's. For Abraham is the father of all who believe."*
> **Romans 4:16 (NLT)**

The focus of "Finding Faith" has been to equip us with knowledge and understanding of how God designed faith as a tool to change the future of our lives.

Change is necessary for improvement. If we don't like what's happening or where we are in life, something will need to change in it before it will get better. First, we need to change our thinking to change our behavior. Next, we need to activate our faith in God by changing our focus from how bad things currently are to thinking about how well things are going to turn out was we are walking in God's will.

We began this book by establishing how important it is to realize that our faith in God is what keeps us moving in the right direction. Faith, like car keys, needs to be used to get our cars (lives) moving so that we can be steered (by God) in the right direction.

We moved on to share how faith isn't as difficult a concept for us to understand as the world believes. We are born into faith. Faith is instinctual. Growing up we have faith we will be fed and clothed. We build our faith as children by believing that we will have a place to live and a safe place to learn and make mistakes. Children aren't taught faith; they just actively exhibit faithful behavior. We should be striving to do the same thing with God as an adult.

We went over why we need faith and why we are always facing problems. Discussing how the enemy is never at a loss for ways to bring trouble to us and how we use our shield of faith as a cover from those fiery darts. We then shared different types of faith and went over how each situation provides different opportunities to exercise our faith. We learned that regardless of our situation, whether it is a car accident or when we are trying to find salvation, we are still using the same type of faith to find the solution.

We discussed salvation because it is the catalyst of faith for believers. Salvation is received by the true belief that Christ died as a substitute for us on the Cross to pay the debt of our sin. Finding faith for Christ is the greatest step we can take towards a brighter future. When we are looking ahead and know that our future is alive in Christ our lives on this Earth can now be looked at with excellence.

Finding faith in God will give us joy, and joy cannot be expressed without a belief that God's plan for our future is brighter than our past. There are no people on this Earth who have joy in their lives today who don't also have plans for their future. If we don't have something to look forward to, we cannot truly have joy in our lives.

As a believer, we should be looking forward to meeting and being in front of Jesus Christ. This alone is enough to keep us looking forward for the rest of our lives. No matter what comes our way we can be encouraged and find peace that at least we have the great gift of eternal life in the presence of God the Father, God the Son, and God the Holy Spirit to look forward to.

We learned how to find faith for today during the moments when we are facing hard times in our present life. Learning why we face trouble is a key to staying active in faith. We talked about practical ways to stay positive today as well as how we should not focus on the trouble tomorrow has in store. We now know that we can do nothing to change the fact that problems come to us. What we can change is how we deal with those problems!

Finally, we discussed how if we have peace on our heart than we will know that our faith in God is active and present in our lives.

Heavenly peace is a gift from God and having it is the sure sign that our faith in Him is working. Gifts from God are given freely and without payment, but we can ask for them. Heavenly peace is a gift we can receive through prayer, and we should constantly be laying our problems at God's feet. When we give our problems to God to take care of then we will be able to receive heavenly peace and know we have found our faith.

We have learned how valuable and precious faith is. It is special to God, and it is the only currency we have to see His will done in our lives. We know we all want to have hope, and there is no hope without faith. We now know how vital faith is to each one of us, and if we have lost faith in God in a particular area, we should be striving to find it.

While we have discussed different ways to find faith and many of the practical methods to activate it, the most important pieces of information we can take from this book are the promises of God. The promises God has made to us about faith, how it works, and what it will do for us are unbreakable and designed to give us great hope.

God's promises are forever, and they will *always* be true. God tells us many things about faith and even though God may use this book to strengthen us in certain areas of our lives, His promises will strengthen us in *all* areas of our life, guaranteed! God's promises are binding, eternal, and can bring hope for a better future to all that seek Him out and ask for one.

God's Promises for Finding Faith

"And now that you belong to Christ, you are the true children of Abraham. You are his heirs, and God's promise to Abraham belongs to you." **Galatians 3:29 (NLT)**

Finding faith can always start and end with God's Word. When we promise someone something, we give him/her our word that we will come through for them. The promises a man gives through his word will sometimes go unfulfilled because of our selfish sin nature and inability to see the future to know for certain that they will succeed. However, the promises of God's Word will always come true. God cannot lie and God watches over His Word. He created the world and everyone in it. God knows how everything begins and will end. When God says He will do something it *will* be done. We can all put our faith in the promises of God.

The following scriptures are just some of those promises. When scriptures are spoken out loud they bring God into our life over that matter. A promise is something we know *He will* do. Find faith in God's Word, and you will find a future full of peace, joy, and hope!

He promises to hear and answer our prayers.

"O people of Zion, who live in Jerusalem, you will weep no more. He will be gracious if you ask for help. He will surely respond to the sound of your cries." **Isaiah 30:19 (NLT)**

He promises Jesus is His Son.

> *"He is the one who will build a Temple to honor my name. He will be my son, and I will be his father. And I will secure the throne of his kingdom over Israel forever."* **1 Chronicles 22:10 (NLT)**

He promises salvation is found through Jesus.

> *"He will swallow up death forever! The Sovereign LORD will wipe away all tears. He will remove forever all insults and mockery against his land and people. The LORD has spoken! In that day the people will proclaim, "This is our God! We trusted in him, and he saved us! This is the LORD, in whom we trusted. Let us rejoice in the salvation he brings!"* **Isaiah 25:8-9 (NLT)**

He promises the power of the Holy Spirit.

> *"I baptize with water those who repent of their sins and turn to God. But someone is coming soon who is greater than I am--so much greater that I'm not worthy even to be his slave and carry his sandals. He will baptize you with the Holy Spirit and with fire."* **Matthew 3:11(NLT)**

He promises us to give us peace.

> *"I am leaving you with a gift--peace of mind and heart. And the peace I give is a gift the world cannot give. So don't be troubled or afraid."* **John 14:27 (NLT)**

He promises to supply our needs.

> *"Jesus replied, "I am the bread of life. Whoever comes to me will never be hungry again. Whoever believes in me will never be thirsty."* **John 6:35 (NLT)**

He promises we will be like Him and not this world.

> *"And because of his glory and excellence, he has given us great and precious promises. These are the promises that enable you to share his divine nature and escape the world's corruption caused by human desires."* **2 Peter 1:4 (NLT)**

He promises to give us power and endurance to follow His will for our lives.

> *"He gives power to the weak and strength to the powerless. Even youths will become weak and tired, and young men will fall in exhaustion. But those who trust in the Lord will find new strength. They will soar high on wings like eagles. They will run and not grow weary. They will walk and not faint."*
> **Isaiah 40:29–31 (NLT)**

He promises to change us and make us better.

> *"And I will give you a new heart, and I will put a new spirit in you. I will take out your stony, stubborn heart and give you a tender, responsive heart."* **Ezekiel 36:26 (NLT)**

He promises to love us.

> *"Those who accept my commandments and obey them are the ones who love me. And because they love me, my Father will love them. And I will love them and reveal myself to each of them."* **John 14:21 (NLT)**

He promises to be our protector.

> *"God's way is perfect. All the LORD's promises prove true. He is a shield for all who look to him for protection."*
> **2 Samuel 22:31 (NLT)**

He promises us many types of blessings if we walk in His will for our lives.

"You will experience all these blessings if you obey the Lord your God: Your towns and your fields will be blessed. Your children and your crops will be blessed. The offspring of your herds and flocks will be blessed. Your fruit baskets and breadboards will be blessed. Wherever you go and whatever you do, you will be blessed "The Lord will conquer your enemies when they attack you. They will attack you from one direction, but they will scatter from you in seven! "The Lord will guarantee a blessing on everything you do and will fill your storehouses with grain. The Lord your God will bless you in the land he is giving you." **Deuteronomy 28:2–8 (NLT)**

He promises us that faith is all we need to see His will done in our lives.

"Then Jesus said to the disciples, "Have faith in God. I tell you the truth, you can say to this mountain, 'May you be lifted up and thrown into the sea,' and it will happen. But you must really believe it will happen and have no doubt in your heart. I tell you, you can pray for anything, and if you believe that you've received it, it will be yours." **Mark 11:22–24 (NLT)**

"And it is impossible to please God without faith. Anyone who wants to come to him must believe that God exists and that he rewards those who sincerely seek him. **Hebrews 11:6 (NLT)**

"You can pray for anything, and if you have faith, you will receive it." **Matthew 21:22 (NLT)**

"For God loved the world so much that he gave his one and only Son, so that everyone who believes in him will not perish but have eternal life." **John 3:16 (NLT)**

"Trust in the Lord with all your heart; do not depend on your own understanding." **Proverbs 3:5 (NLT)**

"For we live by faith, not by sight." **2 Corinthians 5:7 (NIV)**

"Trust in the Lord and do good. Then you will live safely in the land and prosper. Take delight in the Lord, and he will give you your heart's desires. Commit everything you do to the Lord. Trust him, and he will help you." **Psalm 37: 3-5 (NLT)**

Printed in the United States
By Bookmasters